TERRA NOVA
Field Guide for the Cosmological Revolution

PAMELA EAKINS, Ph.D., D.D.

Pacific Center Library
SanFranciscoBooks.US

Copyright © 2018, 2019 Pacific Center Library
Pacific Center, Box 3191, Half Moon Bay, CA 94019

SANFRANCISCOBOOKS.US

Terra Nova: Field Guide for the Cosmological Revolution
Philosophy/Metaphysics
     ISBN-13: 978-1727806144
     ISBN-10: 172780614X

All Rights Reserved. Please credit the author when quoting from this book.

Cover Art: Pamela Eakins, "The Universe"

Interior Art: "Earth Brother," "Earth Sister" by Joyce Eakins.
With permission of U.S. Games, Inc.

Books by Pamela Eakins
    Tarot of the Spirit
    Kabbalah and Tarot of the Spirit
    The Lightning Papers: 10 Powers of Evolution
    Visionary Cosmology: The New Paradigm
    Mothers in Transition
    The American Way of Birth
    Passages for a Spiritual Birth
    Priestess: 3000 BCE to the Future
    Heart, Breath, and Graceful Movement: The Love Poems
    Wild Voracious Love: The Sonnets
    Cosmic Interiors: A Novel
    Days of Spirit: The Four Journals
        Fire, Water, Air, Earth
    Standing Rock: Water, Oil, Sun and Children
    Blindness and Sight: A Memoir
    To End the War: A Memoir

For Our Mother – in All Her Genders.
For Her Children.
For The Future.

CONTENTS

Join the Cosmological Revolution!	i
"I Come from the Future"	1
The Big Call	7
Original You	12
The Cosmological Field	14
The StarGate Awakening	15
For Thou Art the Tree of Life	17
Your Invitation to Terra Nova	19
Terra Nova and the Tree of Life	20
Tarot of the Spirit and the Tree of Life	23
The Tree of Life in Visionary Cosmology	30
Terra Nova Seminary	34
The Terra Nova Vow	39
The Terra Nova Creed	40
The Terra Nova Code	41
This I Remember	42
The Paradigm of Love	46
My Religion is Love	49
Radiating Love	52
To End the War	53
Prayer: Transformation of the Universe	55

The Sacred Temple	57
Walk in Beauty	58
Lobbing Fireballs	59
Become a Terra Nova Center	61
About the Author	67
Photo Montage	69

JOIN THE COSMOLOGICAL REVOLUTION!

Have you longed to deepen in Cosmic Soul,
learn a new language for the future of the Earth,
take down the walls that divide, and open the vortex to Love?
Have you desired to serve your galaxy as a
Celebrant of the Sacred Universe?

If so, then this Field Guide is for You.

Terra Nova: Field Guide for the Cosmological Revolution
offers a foundational paradigm for conscious awakening.
Rooted in the Tree of Life, which branches through the Universe,
the *Terra Nova Field Guide* details three layered iterations of the
wisdom that rends the veil:
Tarot of the Spirit, Visionary Cosmology,
and the Terra Nova Teachings.
Our intent, with this work, is to contribute to the
leap in consciousness, currently breaking,
and centered all across our Earth.

We are legions of Becoming.

We invite you to join with us – to enter the Terra Nova Creed and
Code, and to take the Terra Nova Vow – and become part of our
Cosmological Revolution.
The Terra Nova Field Guide elucidates everything you need to know
to become a member of the Terra Nova Alliance.

You may also become a Planetary Teacher.

For more information on joining our Alliance,
becoming a certified Teacher, or opening your own
Official Terra Nova Center, we invite you to read this book.

www.pamelaeakins.net
www.tarotofthespirit.com
www.pacificmysteryschool.com

PAMELA EAKINS

PAMELA EAKINS

"I COME FROM THE FUTURE"

This book is meant to define "Terra Nova," to explain the meaning of the concept, and to provide guidance and templates to facilitate a philosophical opening. For this book, attempting to be concise, I have skimmed cream off the top of my other books. I invite you to delve deeper into any passage herein by reading the original work as cited.

As I sit down to write, it comes to me strongly, again, that the Next Frontier for humanity is, and will be, rending the veil of consciousness. It is not that I have found "The Way" to do this, but I have, for most of my life, been working on tools that, taken together, do constitute A Process.

This is A Process for creating Social Change.

This is A Process for helping to "jump" our species into a Transmutation.

I realize those are big words – yet they ring true for me. It also rings true for me that I "came in to help save the world." I chuckle at the grandness of that, and, yet, it feels so right.

Early on in my adult life, I became a Sociologist to try to understand why people act as they/we do: why we fight each other, why we hurt each other. At the University of Colorado and Stanford University, I taught the Sociology of Health and Illness: first Mental Health, then Physical, and, later, Spiritual. Sometime during that process, I also became a Priestess, a Kabbalist, a Tarotist, a Minister of Love, a Visionary Cosmologist, and a writer. Through my studies, I discovered that humans, though still with the basic Cro-Magnon brain, *are* capable of mutation, however mutation in humans – so far – is different from much of the mutation we have witnessed on this planet. Humans, for example, haven't yet "grown fins" to adapt. As I point out in my books *The Lightning Papers: Ten Powers of Evolution* and *Visionary Cosmology: The New Paradigm,* the way humans mutate is through ideas. Big ideas, such as farming, the domestication of animals, and ownership of land, have changed the course of our species around the globe. I realized, early on, the importance of Ideas – and early on, I started my search for ideas that might relate to a leap in human consciousness.

"Why spend your time trying to save the world?" you might ask. "That's impossible. Futile. This is the way it is, and it's always been like this." "Maybe," I might answer, "maybe so." But, I now confess to you that, with all my heart and soul, I believe that humans could take a different course.

"Mom," says my son, "things are fine the way they are. *You* don't need to change things. And, who are you to even think that things *should* change?" Well, yes, that is a hard one to answer. Who *am* I to even have such thoughts?

All I can say is that this strange work is my *calling*. I have never been able to get this quest out of my mind. I feel like I am one of the people called to examine human ideas, one of the people called to try to see things differently, one of the people called to try to bring in new philosophy.

And, I am not alone on this path. There must be thousands of us, or, on this planet of close to eight billion people, perhaps we are more than millions.

A lot of us refer to our work as the Call to Awaken.

I was waking up in earnest when I was writing my book *Priestess: Woman as Sacred Celebrant,* later titled, *Priestess: 3000 BCE to The Future.* When I wrote the book I was preparing for my Ordination as a Minister of Love. My teacher had asked me to contemplate the question, "What was the single most important event in the early Christian Church that removed the goddess-oriented religious base and replaced it with a father-orientation?" Well, that was a confounding question that took me on a ride far into the past as well as into the future. To answer that question required both a tremendous amount of research as well as a visionary journey. Though I was not able to answer the question absolutely definitively,

I did realize the profundity of the question itself. That so-called "father-orientation" was one of the ideas, for example, that had "mutated" human consciousness, and, concomitantly, human social structure.

Along the way, as I carried out the writing of *Priestess,* I had a powerful, visceral Vision of myself "emanating from another star system" with the goal of "impacting the philosophy and values of the Earth community." I experienced the surety that I had lived on Earth for over five thousand years – in order to deeply understand what it means to be human. Inside the Vision, I had a sense of timelessness – as in a dream. Perhaps the Vision took place in the past, perhaps in the future. Yet, in the beginning as in the end, Time was not the issue. But the issue was, and is, the question of human potential. Humans are capable of living in every way imaginable. Humans have the potential to cherish and to create synergistically; humans have the potential to disconnect and to destroy. My Mission, as I was to discover, was to contribute to human glory in the arena of bolstering the sense of human interconnection and the understanding of the interrelatedness of All That Is.

As I was researching the material for *Priestess,* I began to hear a Voice speaking to me – as if from another solar system. The Voice said, "When you know how you came to be as you are, you will be able to build a firm base of clear knowledge from which to work. You will have clear insight and presence of mind. You will realize what aspects of the Earth World can and cannot be controlled. Your success will be based on your ability to change that which is changeable and to detach from that which cannot be moved. You will attain the power of initiative through knowing what has been. Through understanding what has been, the nature, depth and mutability of what is will be made perfectly clear. When you understand the nature of the present, you will also know the nature of the future. The present results from what has been. The future is born from what is. When you come into the full realization of this, you will be able to fulfill your mission."

The Voice said that Earth is viewed as one of the most visually entrancing dimensions in the system. The Garden Planet. Small, but full of majesty. Exquisitely sensual. An olfactory feast. Vibrant, verdant. Mysteriously alive. That is partly why I chose to come. I chose to defend the ancient mountains, shifting deserts, rolling plains, tropical and icy seas, skies of the most astonishing pink, lavender, orange, baby blue, cobalt and turquoise, aurora borealis. Glaciers. Volcanoes. Winds that uproot trees. Creatures with wings and fins, fur. Flowers that unfold by day and night, giving off fragrances that entice the heart to love. A planet of dualities elsewhere unknown. Hundreds of nations with plans, hopes, and dreams. The quintessential experiment.

"Throughout the system," the Voice said, "all beings realize that the Earth World's existence is threatened. That anger, greed, recklessness, technological excess, and production-oriented intervention in natural processes threaten to destroy the sphere. Technical intervention and war. The battle for resources. Values clashing values. That is why critical philosophical reflection is so important at this time."

"Now," I was told, "You, like the Sisters and Brothers with whom you left here, must awaken. One by one, stationed all over the Earth, you will remember your origins and begin to pursue your missions. Your mission is to affect the philosophy and values of the Earth World, dear Sister. You chose this mission yourself, of your own free will. Do not focus on the outcome of this work, but attend to the process of creation. Be with the process. Enact the drama of your current life as if it matters. Seek peace, balance, and considered action. Begin to rise to the task before you by observing the lives you have lived, which I will begin to reflect back to you in your next meditation. Observe these lives with detachment. Learn from them, then let any negative effects they have created within you leave your Earthly body. In this way, you will attain wisdom and be freed from the constraints of the past. You will gain the wisdom and understanding of nearly six thousand years of Earth's history. You will begin to understand aspects of the formation of Earth's thought patterns. When you begin to understand these ideas, you will begin to understand the nature of the soul of Life."

That Vision took place in 1993. I was forty years old. Was it *real?* Was I "from somewhere else?" It *seemed* real. Later, I came to understand that it was scientifically "real" in the sense that the Universal Tree of Life has been unfolding for nearly fourteen billion years, the nebulae in our vast Universe, as we now know, are full with the building blocks of life – including amino acids – and, Earth DNA definitely originated in Space. There is no other possibility. Why wouldn't we have such Visions and Memories? No matter how I came to understand it, I felt the urgency of the human threat on our planet coupled with the magnificence of possibilities for our human species – and I could feel my sense of meaning, and the purpose of my life, begin to shift.

Now, fast forward to 2018, twenty-five years later:
Here is the small story I want to open this book with: This past month, I was walking on the bluff-top trail – the same trail on the cliff over the ocean upon which I had originally contemplated the writing of the book *Priestess* – when a neighbor, walking toward me from the opposite direction, suddenly stopped me in the path and began to confront me with an angry tone. He informed me that he had been in military service in the U.S. Navy, that he was a Constitutionalist and a Conservative, and that he was completely in support of the current U.S. President and the President's Administration. He said he believed in a *laissez faire* governmental structure with a heavy emphasis on militarization.

I listened to him – actively. I asked many questions, so that he might expound upon his view – and the reasons he had taken his position. This was not at all the response he expected from me – as he had me pegged for a Liberal, and an enemy.

However, I had learned a few skills along the way which enabled me to "create bridges, not walls." For example, I am a professional Mediator. I am a Counselor. And, I have learned that a major aspect of movement and change involves becoming *receptive,* genuinely receptive. Becoming receptive does not mean becoming manipulative.

Even though he seemed to have been in the mood for a fight and, initially, had chosen me as a target, the more I listened to him and validated him as a thoughtful and conscientious human being, the more he softened. When I expressed appreciation for how well he had thought through his position, when I offered explicit support for the concept of "freedom of expression," and, when I assumed no counter-position, he ended his testimony by saying, "You know, we're not as far apart as I thought we were."

He paused, then, and I thought I might be able to continue my walk, however, it was not that easy. He added, "So, what do *you* think?"

Oh, dear, I thought, *think fast.* Out walking and "communing with Nature," I really had not expected such an encounter in the first place. I do know, though, that, at all times, we must "be ready for anything."

"Wait a minute," I said, "I wasn't expecting that question. Give me a minute." I closed my eyes and quickly "prayed" (sought direction from my "Higher Self," my "Guides," "God," by whatever name you choose). Suddenly, I got a very clear insight. I opened my eyes wide, looked straight into his mischievous blue eyes, and raised up my hands beside my head, palms out, facing him – as in a blessing. In an otherworldly voice, as if I were an Alien-From-Another-Planet, I said, haltingly, "I Come to You from The Future."

At that, we both laughed.

Then I told him that I wasn't a huge fan of the way the Democrats and Republicans had been operating. I told him that, as for myself, I "sit around" spending a lot of time trying to "think up" new ideas. I told him I was trying to "think up stuff" that might help us transcend our current ways of understanding, ideas by which we might become united.

He liked that a lot. He said, "Hmm. We're way closer than I thought."

That made us both laugh.

In fact, we were smiling a lot.

After his proclamation of friendship, we continued on our ways – closer to each other than we had ever imagined, and happier than we had been before our "confrontation."

What happened here? What was the key?

The key was the recognition that, whatever our politics, we need to transcend a social and moral order that no longer seems viable. At least, for many of us, the current social order seems incompatible with the care and feeding of The Future.

What happens when we shift our perspective?

What happens when we "take a leap" and view our social systems from a different perspective?

Excerpts from *Priestess: 3000 BCE to The Future,* p. 16-18.

THE BIG CALL

TERRA NOVA:
New Ground
New Thought
New Frontier
New Earth

Welcome to Terra Nova. Welcome to the Journey of Being Becoming. May the Universal Power of All That Has Been, Is, and Shall Be offer you both Mystery and Home. You are of this Universal Power, this Consciousness, this Knowing. You Are; I Am. Our Mission, together, is to become Creators of the Field and Stewards of the Garden. Together, we are waking up. Together, we are evolving our human consciousness. Together, we are evolving the sensibilities of our species in and as our Earth Community.

Why is this important *now?* First and foremost, because we have realized we are in a New Place and a New Time. We have realized that the Universe is not "up there" somewhere, not "out there" somewhere, but within and all around us. Things are not like we thought they were when we believed the Earth was flat with a bowl of stars overhead. Things are not like we thought when we believed our Milky Way was the only galaxy in existence. Things have changed – and very recently – as far as our understanding goes.

In 1923, for example, with the new Hubble telescope, we realized, for the very first time, there was a galaxy beyond our own Milky Way. What we thought was a nebula turned out to be our Sister Galaxy, Andromeda! *We were not alone!* We *are* not alone – and that discovery was less than one hundred years ago. My grandmothers were just blossoming as young women in the Roaring Twenties. Think of that: up until that moment, we seemed to be an isolated planet.

And, our planet had seemed large. Upon our planet, all the kings and queens and wars had "happened," all the exploration, colonization, the discovery of gold and oil and electricity and antibiotics, the invention of telephones and writing and the printing press and the canoe, and the domestication of fire: just *Everything*.

But, the view of Andromeda up close was only the beginning of a new perspective. Now we know we live in a universe (or a multiverse) with billions and billions of galaxies, and there is no end in sight. We live on a tiny planet in a tiny solar system – a realm of no up and no down – which gives us a brand new sense of Place, and Space and Time, and that changes Everything.

Here, then, is a paradox: Our planet is so tiny against the vast backdrop of Space, it seems insignificant. As Carl Sagan said, when you get out just a little way, Earth is just a "pale blue dot." And, against the vast stretch of geologic time, our lives, in their brevity, also seem miniscule and pale. And, yet, even as we become acutely aware that our "Spaceship Earth" is but a nearly invisible dot, we simultaneously realize that dot is glorious! She is a Living Planet! And, what's more, not only are we hers, she's all we've got.

Even as, on July 20, 1969, we saw "our Mother's" portrait broadcast for the first time from the Moon, we became *motivated* by her smallness. We became motivated by her beauty – for she is a rare blue pearl, for she is a sparkling sapphire, for she is our planet of blue sky and *water* and all those miraculous ecosystems and species. She is our amazing biosphere! We felt compelled to cry out: Let us Celebrate Earth's Magnificence! Let us become Reverent! Exactly because, with our new sense of Place, Space and Time, we realized that not only is the Universe not as we thought it was, but *we* are not who we *thought* we were either. Against that view from the Moon, a lot of human activities – war, for example – began to seem quite senseless – and, yet, what else might we *do?* And *that* thought began to usher in a whole new dimension of the Call – not that we could yet understand the implications, or the way forward. We just *knew* – in our bones – things had changed.

One American soldier, drafted in later years to fight in the war in Vietnam said: "All the people coming over here now are a lot different than they used to be… World War Two type people are the old Vietnam people. Now, it's the Woodstock generation coming to Vietnam." The Woodstock Music Festival concluded on August 17, 1969 – less than a month after we flew to the Moon, less than a month after we witnessed, with eyes wide open, The Great Truth.

Today, we sense a Big Call. It is a Call to think differently, even if we can't make out clearly what that means or what it might entail. In some sense, this is a spiritual Call and a spiritual challenge, involving all our sensibilities. Our Big Call applies to the way we reconceptualize, reinterpret, and reformulate our understanding of our Universe – both outer and inner. As we create our meanings anew, our sense of purpose transforms.

What we are learning is that what we think, say, and do matters. Our Future depends on our process. And, as we are carried by our planet, our planet, concomitantly, carries on within the realm of our understanding. Therefore, our thinking matters. Our ideas matter. And, given the influx of possibilities, what we choose to believe makes all the difference in the world.

Terra Novan and Psychotherapist, Donna Blethen, wrote:

A CALLING

From above,
Outside the sphere of here
There are a hundred billion leagues
Beyond time, beyond space
A grandfather message
A Calling.

Stretch past the veneer of culture and tradition.
Reach as far as you can.
Fasten onto the great unknowing.
Do not let the awful cramping of fear

Make you think you are limited.
Pray.
Pray.
Go into prayer night and day.
Reach
Breach
Go beyond the banks.
Bring back a universal wisdom that is timeless.

Climb to the pinnacle,
Plunge into the depths.
Do not keep silent, private, hidden.
Open up.
Share what you learn.
Bring others along.
Coin whatever phrases will win over the heart
The heart of the matter
The heart of the listener.

Tell the story to reassure the ears.
Create the vision that changes sight.
Do not we all need to see differently?
The wisdom learned on your journey will guide others on theirs.

You dare to advance on the path.
Look back.
There is a runway of starlight shimmering to make the voyage safer for others.
Remember it is the remembering
Coming back to the great unity of love from which we all came.

Do not be afraid.
The words will come, the images will arise, the feelings will pulse.
Just commit to the journey
Do the work of believing.

> You have worthy fellow travelers.
> All of you will hold each other
> Pick each other up
> Bring each other to new expanses.
>
> Like the currents through the ocean kelp
> A way is always found.
> That is our promise to you:
> To live to your greatest potential.
> With that commitment we bring you unity and love in all their myriad forms.
> None is greater than the other.
> All are worthy, unique, and part of the cosmic web.

So, then, let us heed the Big Call. Let us begin our Journey by breaking open our own Consciousness. Let us begin by entering into the Cosmological Imagination. Let us begin with the realization that we *are* Cosmos. We, ourselves, are Universe in the making. We are the Universal Tree of Life unfolding. And we *do* hold the Power of Creation.

Do you see?

This, my Friend, does herald a Cosmological Revolution.

ORIGINAL YOU

Here is where begin: You were born into, out of, *as* and *of* our Universe. You are, what I call, "Centrated Universal Original Being." That means: You evolved out of the Origin of All That Is. You emerged in your Moment – your Time and Place – as absolutely Original You. Implicitly and explicitly, you are a Center of Universal Origination, a Zone of Universal Emergence. You are an Original, Originating Center of Universe evolving. You are Universe creating the future of its own becoming.

It took 13.73 billion years of universal artistry for our Universe, creating, combining and recombining its elements and energies, to evolve into You. Composed of millions of atoms of oxygen, carbon, hydrogen, nitrogen, calcium and phosphorus, You are the very essence of the centrated – centrally-combined and focused – state-of-the-art Universe being and becoming. You are creative Universe at the cutting edge of its own existence.

Since each of your atoms is predominantly composed of space, 99.9 % space and 0.1% matter, you are predominantly made of the all-originating Panoriginal Field of the Universe concentrated into a spacious creative unit. Do you see? You are the very essence of Universe and Space-Time itself. You are Originating Universe focused into its own Center "walking."

Further, 99.9% of you develops according to the genetic code for "human" which is part and parcel of the DNA code for our home planet. (DNA provides the genetic instructions or "blueprint" for development, functioning and information storage in living organisms.) Even though you share 99.9% of the same DNA as all other human beings, the 0.1% of the DNA code that makes you unequivocally YOU, makes you *absolutely original*. The You that exists right now, in this present moment, has never been before and will never be again.

The context you were born into is original. Your talents are original. Your desires are original. You are a centrated unit of Universe, a centrated being, being and *becoming* in every moment. You are state-of-the art Universe engaging in its own fascinating cosmological quest.

You are Universe even as You are *a* Universe concentrating Creation.

You are at the Center of the Universe and the Universe is centering upon You, right now. Not only are you a Center of the Universe, but you, yourself, are a Universe within Universes and also a point of Origin. Though You have never been before and will never be again, you are nonetheless constituted of the limitless, boundless and immortal Universe ever in the process of its continuing evolution. The potential of your becoming was present at the Origin of the Universe. You originated as an Original Being which, in turn, is capable of origination. As Living Universe centrating within its own being, you are Universe in the process of creating its own becoming. You are sowing the seeds of the unfolding future. The future you originate will unfold within and all around you. Simply because you *are,* your region of the enveloping Universe is forever changed.

You emerge in this world as a gift of Universe. The Universe has focused intensively for 13.73 billion years to bring You about. You are the Universe awakening into the mystery of its own creation, the mystery of its own potential, the mystery of its own adventure. Your dream is the dream of Universe dreaming – in the unique dimension of Centrated Universe we only know as You.

This is food for thought. This is new ground. New ground is Terra Nova.

From *Visionary Cosmology. The New Paradigm.* p. 21-22..

THE COSMOLOGICAL FIELD

Things are not as we thought they were:

You are an Electromagnetic Field walking through an Electromagnetic Field.

You are Electromagnetic Force.

You are Spiritual Will.

You are a Force to be reckoned with.

You create the conditions of the Field.

And – you are subject to the Field's conditions.

Therefore, sow in right season

And, on winter ice,

use caution.

From *To End the War: A Memoir,* p. 359.

THE STARGATE AWAKENING

I AM the spiritual and material starfield of Universal Life.

I AM the body of the Cosmos in every moment spinning into form and realization.

I AM an electrified forcefield inspired to keep the Universe in motion.

I AM a center of creation and a zone of cosmological emergence.

I AM a sanctuary of nurturance.

I AM the power of dissolution and dispersion, the change that heralds the new.

I AM integral to the expansive interrelations of the cosmological community.

I AM the cosmological adventure and the transmutation of imagination.

I AM the record of cosmic experience holding, integrating and creating new code.

I AM reflective Universe witnessing and remembering the possibilities of its course.

I AM radiant Cosmos expressing itself as a child risen from Sun.

I AM the StarGate Awakening, the portal and the passage into new dimensions of becoming.

I Am. Thou Art.

I AM.
YOU ARE.
WE ARE.
THEY ARE.

Do you see? You are with me and I am with you.
We are Synergistic Mind awakening in the Infinite Field
of the New Era.

Behold!
You are Living Universe.
The Powers of Creation are in you and with you Now.
Your Offering is your Art.
Take the Leap!

From *Visionary Cosmology: The New Paradigm*, p. 164-165

FOR THOU ART THE TREE OF LIFE

Our Universe evolves as the Living Tree of Life, growing out of the core of its own Being. The core of our Universe is everywhere. The center is everywhere. Everywhere, our Universe concentrates itself to bring itself forth, and, everywhere it brings itself forth, becomes a center of its own becoming.

Thou Art Universe.
Thou Art the Living Tree of Life.

You are a creative Center of the Universe. What you think, say, and do matters, because you are not only the Living Tree of Life of the Universe, you are the future of the Living Tree of Life of the Universe.

You are the seed that falls in the forest.

That seed contains all the forest that has ever been – past, present and future. The seed of you is the ancient forest. The seed of you is the forest yet to come.

You are, and are not, like every seed that has ever been. You are like every seed in that every seed holds – in right circumstance – the potential for growth. At the same time, you are unlike every seed that has ever been, in that, even as each Daughter Cell is not an exact replica of each Mother Cell, you are a seed that carries the Wisdom of Adaptation.

The forest of The Future will contain elements that you, yourself, dream into it – for Thou Art the Living Tree of Life enacting the Cosmological Imagination.

    What story will you tell?
    Upon what dream will you create The Future?
    What will you retain? What will you release?
    What do you value the most?

I maintain that Terra Nova, the New Frontier, the New Land, *could* be a Land of Kindness. I value Kindness – and, right now, with this very thought, this word, this stroke of the key, I am dreaming Kindness into The Future. I am dreaming Kindness into The Forest.
    Will you dream with me?
    Might we enter the Land of Kindness together?
    Might we come home to The Future as a World of Love?

May I enter the Land of Kindness.
May I go there by thought alone.
May I imagine that I might arrive in that rarefied region, and then,
suddenly,
that Field will be my awakening.

See *To End the War: A Memoir,* p. 353.

YOUR INVITATION TO TERRA NOVA

Terra Nova is the Land of Kindness.

Let's enter the Land of Kindness.
Let's go there by thought alone.
Let's imagine that we might arrive in that rarefied region, and then,
suddenly, That Field will be our awakening.
Let us awaken in that brave and ancient land
where caring is the highest value.
Let us realize that that habitation, the Land of Kindness,
is only a dream away.
It is only a breath away.
It is only a heartbeat away, a smile and a loving touch away.

Come with me.
Come with me to the Land of Grace and we will meet in that place
where power is created
by joining together.

Come with me, and we will meet in that place
where we realize, fully
with awe and with wonder, that
We are All Children of the Same Universe.

From *Blindness and Sight: A Memoir,* p. 113.

TERRA NOVA AND THE TREE OF LIFE

Terra Nova: The Land of New Consciousness
Our Mission: To Evolve Our Understanding
Our Vision: A New Model of Interrelationship, Linking Together, and Celebration; a Cosmological Revolution
Our Goal: The Operationalization of Love
Our Means and Method: The Tree of Life

The Tree of Life is a map for navigating the understanding of consciousness. It symbolizes key aspects of cosmological emergence and evolution. As we immerse in the teachings of the Tree, we realize that our consciousness is, at once, individual as well as "cosmic": our consciousness is absolutely unique as well as inextricably intertwined with the universal consciousness in which we continue to "become." Not one of us is separate from the greater consciousness within and all around us. This proclamation – by which I stand – is a Mobius strip of universal truth.

The Tree of Life is a map, as well as a paradigm, for navigating consciousness. According to philosopher Thomas Kuhn, the foremost contributor to the language of paradigm, a paradigm is the model or pattern we are operating by. Our paradigm allows us to determine what seems fitting and right and what seems out of place or anomalous. Our paradigm allows us to determine if there are problems we wish to solve. A paradigm not only highlights problems, it also provides the means or the apparatus by which to formulate solutions.

In *The Structure of Scientific Revolutions* (1962), Thomas Kuhn points out how the paradigm – an internally-consistent set of self-evident "assumptions" – allows us to articulate what is known, and then to expand beyond the "known" via specific forms of exploration and experimentation that are generated directly out of the paradigm itself. As we understand and further articulate the paradigm, we simultaneously discover and articulate our own Vision in our own Voice.

In working with a paradigm, we may become aware that we are, in fact, "living by" a paradigm. A paradigm constitutes a worldview. A worldview may be completely invisible, and so commonplace that it "breathes like air." We may not realize we are breathing that air unless that air becomes tainted. If our survival becomes threatened, we may be more likely to realize the mechanisms of the "operating system" that hold the worldview in place.

The Tree of Life Paradigm – with which we are working in Terra Nova – is believed to have originated as an archetypal ten-point number system in Ancient Egypt. The model was further articulated in Ancient Greece as well as greatly expounded upon by students of Kabbalah through countless generations. It has been preserved and transmitted via the Western Mystery Tradition.

The Ten Spheres of the Tree of Life show how the Cosmos unfolds and also, as an aspect of the Cosmos, how consciousness itself unfolds. In its essence, the pattern of emergence can be described as follows:

THE TREE OF LIFE PARADIGM
1. Everything originates from the origin, is original, originates, and gives rise to the original. At the same time, due to universal expansion, everything that originates becomes the center of the Universe.
2. The Universe is a charged field wherein aspects are drawn together as well as propelled apart.
3. The Universe gives birth to further articulations of its own existence.
4. The Universe organizes and builds systems to sustain itself.
5. The Universe deconstructs, breaks down and reconstitutes.

6. The Universe is in the continual process of balancing forces and forms and seeking harmonious equilibrium.
7. The Universe continually evolves and adapts to changes within its own being.
8. The Universe develops codes, formulae, and symbols by which it systematically creates, sustains, destroys, and remembers.
9. The Universe absorbs and contains its own experience in the personal and collective "storehouse" which may be seen or unseen.
10. The Universe, in all dimensions, emits what it absorbs according to its nature, both "domesticated" and "wild."

The Tree of Life Paradigm is said to be a "living paradigm" in that it is not a fixed set of conclusions, but a *process* that is constantly evolving. Each individual studying this paradigm – from his or her own unique perspective – has the power to transmit the "model" in a newly altered form. As we study the Tree of Life, we are studying a *pattern of emergence* – even as we simultaneously awaken into the power and efficacy of our own, very personal, experience.

It is said that, as you immerse in the Tree of Life Paradigm, you, yourself, become the Vehicle, the Passenger, the Path, the Vision, and the Voice. You begin to realize that you, yourself, are the ancient of ancients and the holy of holies. You, yourself, are a cosmological being from the heart of the Universe. You are a magical, wild, original enterprise with the power to alter the course of the future. You are Universe itself in the process of its own creation; creativity creating for the sheer joy of experiencing the possibilities of its own existence. You begin to realize that you hold within you all the sacred powers of the living Cosmos. In fact, You *are* the Tree of Life.

The powers of the Tree of Life – which constitute the operating system of Terra Nova – are your birthright. You are the cosmological miracle of the Tree in the process of its own awakening. You are Life *alive* in its task. What will you dream? How will you become?

See *Kabbalah and Tarot of the Spirit,* p. 14-15.

TAROT OF THE SPIRIT AND THE TREE OF LIFE

For many decades, I have been a student and teacher in the Western Mystery Tradition. Throughout that period, I have relied heavily on the Tree of Life Paradigm – the basis of the Western Mystery Tradition – to create all my works. This is especially true for *Tarot of the Spirit*.

Tarot of the Spirit, an extensive articulation of the Tree of Life paradigm, underlies the operating system of Terra Nova. Terra Nova is nothing less than the "new frontier" we are seeking for our species. I believe that the Tree of Life Paradigm, as elucidated by *Tarot of the Spirit*, holds the promise of personal and social transformation – the promise of the Cosmological Revolution – through providing a symbolic language with the power to transmute what we "think into" our world.

The Tree of Life Paradigm, as articulated in *Tarot of the Spirit*, is the same Tree of Life Paradigm that is contained within, and elucidated by, all Western Mystery Schools. The paradigm consists of the ten points/spheres of the Tree of Life which bloom into the Ten Powers of the Kabbalah, which are the Ten Powers of Tarot.

The Tree of Life pattern/diagram/glyph can be conveyed very simply by three triangles and a dot. Each triangle contains three points or spheres, each of which is a point/power of the paradigm. Thus, the three Triangles, taken together, contain the first nine points/powers of the paradigm. The last point/power, the tenth power, stands alone as the dot at the bottom of the Tree. A simple representation looks something like this:

  The first/upper Triad, called the Supernal or Cosmological Triangle, consists of the first three points or spheres. Spheres 1, 2 and 3 are called Kether, Chokmah and Binah. The second/middle Triad, called the Ethical Triangle, consists of Spheres 4, 5 and 6: Chesed, Geburah and Tiphareth. The third/lower Triad, the Astral or Transformational Triangle, contains Spheres 7, 8 and 9: Netzach, Hod and Yesod. The final point/sphere, Sphere 10, Malkuth, gathers and holds the energies of all the other spheres.
  Following is a numerical representation of the 10 Powers, Points or Spheres of the Tree of Life as depicted in *Tarot of the Spirit*:

```
        1
   3      2
   5      4
        6
   8      7
        9

        10
```

  And, following is the glyph of the Tree of Life completed with its branches or "paths":

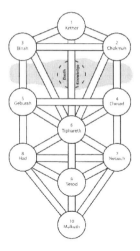

If you know what each point/sphere/power of each Triangle represents, and if you know what the point/sphere/power at the bottom represents, then you can understand the meaning of the Kabbalistic Tree of Life. This is what we learn as we work, play, meditate and study with *Tarot of the Spirit*. The process we use is called "doing pathwork on the Tree of Life."

In short, the ten points of the Kabbalistic Tree of Life (the Ten Powers) become the Ones through Tens of Tarot. So, when you enter into *Tarot of the Spirit* – or any other Kabbalistic Tarot deck – you are entering directly into the Kabbalistic Tree of Life Paradigm and the ancient and futuristic Western Mystery Tradition. When you work with *Tarot of the Spirit,* when you draw any of the Ones through Tens of Fire, Water, Wind or Earth, you are wielding the dynamic ideas and energies of the Terra Nova Paradigm.

You might imagine, as you work with the cards, you are working with a system of flashcards – flashcards containing energies that have the power to catalyze your spirit (Fire), heart (Water), mind (Wind) and body (Earth). The Ten Powers have the capacity to ignite your creativity and enflame your evolution. Working with these Ten Powers, you will be able to create new worlds, within and without.

Following is an encapsulation of the Tree of Life Paradigm as it is interwoven within and throughout *Tarot of the Spirit*:

TAROT OF THE SPIRIT AND THE TREE OF LIFE

0. THE PANORIGINAL FIELD. Panorigination: Space is a Panoriginal Field which continually produces energies and substances everywhere. The Panoriginal Field, at all levels, constitutes all that has been, is, and ever shall be.

1. KETHER. The One of Fire, Water, Air/Wind and Earth: Origination/Centration
    Everything in the Universe has its origins in the beginning of the Universe. Everything is original. Everything originates. The Cosmological Power of Origination/Centration is the state of having been assembled into a One, an original being with the power of origination. You are a centrated, original, universal One.

2. CHOKMAH. The Two of Fire, Water, Air/Wind and Earth: Attraction
    The Cosmological Power of Attraction is the state of being drawn, or drawing, toward, out or into. In physics, the Law of Attraction indicates the mutual action by which bodies or particles of matter tend to draw together and/or cohere. The complex interplay of attractions keeps the whole of the Universe in motion. Your attractions are the process of the Universe becoming. Your attractions initiate the evolution of the One.

3. BINAH. The Three of Fire, Water, Air/Wind and Earth: Creation
    The Cosmological Power of Creation refers not only to the totality of all that is, but to the totality of all that has been and shall be, and all processes – known and unknown – by which all that exists issues forth. The Power of Creation encompasses the concepts of creation, genesis, generation, emergence and evolution. On the basis of simple and complex attractions, aspects of the Universe converge and congeal to bring forth the new. Each One is integral to and critical within this process.

4. CHESED. The Four of Fire, Water, Air/Wind and Earth: Stabilization

> The Cosmological Power of Stabilization is the action by which the Universe secures its creations as well as the ability to continue creating. The Universe stabilizes centers of creativity, zones of emergence, and yet nothing in the Universe is ever completely settled or absolutely stable. Stabilized centers of creativity emerge as staging grounds of what might be called "quivering equilibrium." The process of stabilization is directly related to discernment. The Universe stabilizes what it values. You are a centrated packet of Universe. You might ask yourself: What do you value enough to stabilize?

5. GEBURAH. The Five of Fire, Water, Air/Wind and Earth: Cataclysm

> The Cosmological Power of Cataclysm refers to a great flood or deluge or any great upheaval that causes sudden, potentially disastrous change as in an earthquake or in a war. Whether it happens by chance, as a mechanism to right imbalances, or as part of the intentional flow of the Universe, cataclysm accelerates transformation. There is great value in the practice of accepting and working with the power of cataclysm as it arises —with varying degrees of force – in the course of our day to day lives.

6. TIPHARETH. The Six of Fire, Water, Air/Wind and Earth: Synergy

> The Cosmological Power of Synergy is the combined action of separate agencies, which, when working together, have a greater total effect than the sum of their individual effects. The whole is greater than the sum of its parts. The Universe draws on the power of its parts: the universal community. Through synergistic interactions, the grand processes of the Universe continue to empower creation. We might ask: What is our contribution to the synergistic universal community?

7. NETZACH. The Seven of Fire, Water, Air/Wind and Earth: Transmutation

> The Cosmological Power of Transmutation refers to an overarching change by which one form – condition, nature

or substance — converts, or is converted into, another form. Transmutation applies to everything from atoms to stars to mountains to people. Transmutation implies that some identifiable energy or substance persists through the change, nonetheless the "leap" in condition/s or change in state, is "permanent." Transmutation is a creative surge that initiates the overarching change that calls forth each new era. Activate your imagination to move ever deeper into the creative surge that heralds the new — within and without.

8. HOD. The Eight of Fire, Water, Air/Wind and Earth: Symbolization

> The Cosmological Power of Symbolization is the ability to create an image, sound, or other form of abstraction that represents the Universe or an aspect of the Universe. While the act of creating the symbol may constitute a revelation in itself, symbols also constitute the means of human communication. The Universe remembers its experience through symbolic coding. Creating symbols to encode the experience of the past and present, and/or to create the future — consciously — is a trait inherent in the human species. The symbols you create contain the power to evolve the Cosmos.

9. YESOD. The Nine of Fire, Water, Air/Wind and Earth: Absorption

> The Cosmological Power of Absorption demonstrates how the Universe, or an aspect of the Universe, takes in and incorporates, assimilates or reacts *with*. The Universe absorbs and retains knowledge even as it evolves. As humans, we retain our experience — past, present, and future — in symbolic systems, in our cultural storehouses of knowledge, and in our collective and individual consciousness and "unconscious." We can consciously and actively select what experiences we wish to absorb and how we wish to absorb and transform them, in order to participate in creating the perceptions and the future we hold possible in our personal and collective imagination. What will we focus on? What do we choose to absorb?

10. MALKUTH. The Ten of Fire, Water, Air/Wind and Earth: Radiance
> The Cosmological Power of Radiance is the way the Universe, or an aspect of the Universe, emerges and radiates from and into the Panoriginal Field. The Universe shines. You shine as the Universe.

For intensive study in Tarot of the Spirit, read Tarot of the Spirit, *and* Kabbalah and Tarot of the Spirit. *You can also become a student in our online Tarot/Kabbalah Mystery School:*
> www.tarotofthespirit.com
> www.pacificmysteryschool.com

The above writings on the Tarot as the Tree of Life Paradigm are from *Kabbalah and Tarot of the Spirit,* p. 53-58.

THE TREE OF LIFE IN VISIONARY COSMOLOGY

We have traveled into space, looked upon our small, brave planet twirling like a star sapphire in a black velvet field, and we have learned a truth. The Universe is not only "out there" but "in here." Not only are we are made of Universe, but we are self-reflective Universe in the process of its own becoming. We are wholly creative and we are *alive*.

Science bequeaths us with gift after gift, in every moment laying precious jewels at our feet, but we are still stumbling on the path. We get so overwhelmed, we imagine we don't even belong on our planet – that we are somehow alien in our own land.

All this is symptomatic of being inside a paradigm shift. The way we thought it was is no longer. Here is some background: a paradigm spells out The Way It Is: how and why things work. It offers members of a world 1) a belief system and a basis for commitment, 2) symbols that are understood and used with little questioning or dissent, 3) preferred analogies and metaphors, and 4) a common set of values by which community is created. A paradigm holds a world together. But, when big new insights generate big new questions, cracks appear in the matrix. The paradigm can come tumbling down. That's when revolutions occur – which is where we are today: inside a revolution in consciousness.

The newly-emerging paradigm of Visionary Cosmology, based on the Tree of Life, integrates our worldview in a whole new way. Steeped in state-of-the-art science, we arrive at a new and comprehensive understanding of our state-of-the-art selves. This, in turn, activates our new mission: to become Cultural Creatives in the Living Field of Evolution. That's what the enterprise of Terra Nova is all about.

Here are some definitions:

> Visionary: unusual foresight; existing in imagination; dreaming the future; seeing visions; a seer.

> Cosmology: the study of the cosmos; the nature of the Universe: origins, structures, space-time relations.

> Visionary Cosmology: a meta-cosmology integrating state-of-the-art science and state-of-the-art self into a brand new story: a narrative with the power to imbue meaning and instigate change.

Visionary Cosmology shows us a new way to know a new world. That new world is the essence of Terra Nova. We begin to know the new world with a journey into outer space which takes us, concurrently, deep into the heart of our very own interior. Along the way we fall in love and give birth to whole new imaginings. We learn how to create sanctuary and navigate chaos. We become a refuge of wisdom, fully at home where we are, armed with codes, oracles, and fully-activated powers.

Visionary Cosmology lives at the thriving intersection of science and spirituality. In my book *Visionary Cosmology: The New Paradigm*, I show how the Tree of Life Paradigm creates the underlying structure and process by which we can begin to integrate scientific discoveries with newly emerging consciousness.

The following chart from *Visionary Cosmology: The New Paradigm* demonstrates how employing the Tree of Life Paradigm, the same paradigm that upholds the structure of the Western Mystery Tradition and *Tarot of the Spirit,* can help us to understand and shift our perceptions from one set of assumptions and conclusions into another:

VISIONARY COSMOLOGY.
TOWARD A NEW PARADIGM
THE TEN COSMOLOGICAL POWERS OF EVOLUTION

POWER	INDUSTRIAL MIND	SYNERGISTIC MIND
1. CENTRATION Definition of Self	The universe is "out there." I am a stranger here: alone, isolated, alienated.	I belong here. I am made of universe. I am universe evolving.
2. ATTRACTION Our Aspirations	Desire based on insecurity, fear, and the need for belonging	Recognition of, and taking responsibility for, innate cosmological gifts
3. CREATION Our Imagination	Imagining and creating a world that rewards individual achievement at any price	Imagining and creating an integrated/integral world that cherishes, sustains, and celebrates diversity
4. STABILIZATION Our Values	Evolving security systems to protect valuables	Evolving security systems to promote happiness
5. CATACLYSM Our Methods	Enforcement of values through violence and war	Collective, love-based responses to suffering
6. SYNERGY Our Systems	Short-sighted product and profit-based focus which disregards the integral health of the Earth and the Earth communities	Long-sighted process-based focus; success is defined as participating with diverse Earth communities to create vibrantly healthy life
7. TRANSMUTATION Our Responses	Coping, "numbing out" or escaping with substances, television, video games, etc.	Seeking deeper meaning; living a vitally alive day-to-day visionary experience
8. SYMBOLIZATION Our Institutions	Systematizing, institutionalizing, and reproducing dysfunctional patterns	Imagining ever new ways of being and becoming; creating a new symbology for continuing evolution
9. ABSORPTION Our Internalized Personal and Collective Values	Internalization of personal and collective values which have the power to deny both the self and the greater Earth communities	Internalization of personal and collective values that honor, celebrate, heal and sustain the self and the greater Earth communities
10. RADIANCE Our Sensibilities	Living a "dimmed-down" life; potential feeling of alienation or "anomie" (occupying a culturally-ineffective "roleless role"); sense of "disconnect" or apathy	Radiating cosmological beauty; efficacious participation in human culture and destiny within the greater cosmological community; an inalienable sense of belonging

Terra Nova is, simultaneously, a realm and a quest. It is New Consciousness with the explicit task of actively seeking to move away from the destructive potential of Industrial Consciousness and into the healing potential of Synergistic Consciousness.

It is, in short, no less than a Cosmological Revolution.

You can become a Certified Visionary Cosmologist by studying the book Visionary Cosmology: The New Paradigm, *answering the questions at the end of each chapter, and submitting your answers. With deep immersion, you might find that your thinking about the fit between science and spirituality has become revolutionized.*

Reading The Lightning Papers: Ten Powers of Evolution *will be critically transformative in this regard.*

Please contact Pamela Eakins for detailed information on becoming a Visionary Cosmologist: and, potentially, teaching in the program as part of the Terra Nova Alliance: www.pamelaeakins.net

The above writing on paradigm shift is from *Visionary Cosmology: The New Paradigm,* p. xiv; p. 98.

TERRA NOVA SEMINARY

Terra Nova: New Ground
Seminary: Seedbed

The Terra Nova Seminary Teachings are new and experimental. Based on the understanding offered by the Tree of Life Paradigm, as elucidated in *Tarot of the Spirit* and *Visionary Cosmology,* the Terra Nova Seminary is an attempt to seed the space-time ground of Being – the Planetary Field – with new dimensions of Love, Peace and Art. All of the students who enter – from everywhere around the world – are actively engaged in expanding the scope of the Cosmological Revolution.

In Terra Nova, Love is operationalized as compassion, sympathy, empathy, understanding, sensitivity, witnessing, and participating in the heart and soul of the Living Cosmos. Love entails the practices of appreciation and blessing. Ultimately, living in Love is living inside of a state of grace, within and without.

Peace is operationalized as serenity, tranquility, flowing naturally within and between dimensions, as well as attaining and mobilizing expertise in non-violent communication and conflict transformation.

Art is operationalized as action, movement, cause, creation, and active celebration of the Sacred Universe, comprising and surrounding All That Is. Art is healing. Healing is Art.

The Terra Nova Seminary is a radical departure from what we normally think of as priest/priestess/ministerial studies. From beginning to end, though students develop their own belief systems, all of us begin with this: 1) You are living, self-reflective Universe on the path of its own becoming, and, 2) We are all children of the same

Universe.

Terra Nova goes beyond interfaith and nondenominational. In our Terra Nova quest, we activate a Love Story with the Cosmos. Even as we study ancient stories about the creation and emanation of our Universe, we explore state-of-the-art science with the principles of Visionary Cosmology. In the end, we come to know ourselves, our ancestors, and our descendents, as living Gaia. We come to realize that the whole of the Universe is alive – and we are That. We are the Cosmic Tree of Creation, the Living Tree of Life.

In Terra Nova, we use the Tree of Life Paradigm as the scaffolding for studying *Tarot of the Spirit, Visionary Cosmology,* and World Spirituality. Employing the One through Ten pattern of the Tree of Life Paradigm, as part of our studies we enter into classes on Universal Soul, the Sacred Masculine, the Divine Feminine, the Cosmic Love Story, the World's Religions, the New Earth, Crises and Collapse, Death and Grieving, and Nonviolent Conflict Transformation. Each student completes the work understanding their own unique Offering, Quest, Oracle, Cause, and Code. Our purpose is knowing the Self. Concomitantly, our purpose is understanding the "Other." Our purpose is synergistic unity. Our purpose is appreciation and celebration.

Along the way, we experience Ten Ceremonies of Empowerment, which are instrumental to growing the Soul.

Priestess Maia Whitemare, in the beginning of our studies, wrote a prayer for Terra Nova: "In the city of convention, in the closed places where judgment lives and prospers, let there be opening, let there be healing, love and play. I am asking: Help me to have the will, the strength, the wisdom to banish the illness of apathy. Let me have the courage to seek and support the liberation of myself and humanity's soul. Help me to have the heart, mind and spirit to allow the coming of the fire of life lived as universal love song, the song of becoming that which needs to be born, needs to be One with Cosmic Light."

At the end of our studies, upon witnessing our Graduation and Ordination, poet Cheryl Ban wrote:

PAMELA EAKINS

ORDINATION

White Roses filled the room

Ten woman stood,
waiting for years for this moment,
or so they thought

How would they know

studying, reading, writing…
was preparing the mind

How would they know

when they spoke their vows
…ancestors were listening

How would they know

Their Beloved Teacher was
carrying The Spark
of those who walked before,
who also had made vows
to serve Love

How would they know

The Ancestors had been
looking through the centuries for
A Beacon of Heart Love,
found Her…
Shining

Humble
… to the long Lineage

Though not Innocent ……

She knows of the Flame that burns
Deep, the Cross to carry,
A Heart's beating Call
Once heard,

TERRA NOVA

Is forever known

How would they know

Their bodies would accept or reject
what the mind so carefully had chosen

Fragrant White Roses

Rose petals knew
what was gathering in the currents of time

Their Teacher, the Bishop Priestess,
had become the lineage's torch,
to light the flame
of the Woman who now stood

innocent
before Her

Head bowed,
Crown exposed,
Ancient Hands,
…firmly held…
until the Flame
was alight and
burning

Trinity complete

Now They Knew
what the rose petals knew.

Our Graduation and Ordination Ceremony is something like a wedding. People are ordained by their own personal vows along with the Terra Nova Vow – which you will see in the passage that follows.

Our Terra Novans said that a wedding requires "Something Old, Something New, Something Borrowed, and Something Blue." For Something Old, we exalted the Tree of Life Paradigm, passed down to us for so many centuries. For Something New, we heralded Terra Nova itself. For Something Borrowed, we celebrated the wonderful aspects of each of the world's religions, even as we sought for the shared Wisdom therein. Love seemed to be the key. Love seemed to be our answer. For Something Blue – well, that was easy – we would celebrate our Blue Planet, the Mother from whom we emerged, our small planet Earth. Blue is also the color of the Divine Feminine, the color of the Cosmic Sea reflecting the Cosmic Sky. Blue is Water Mother, the very essence of Compassion reflecting the power of Wisdom. All of that knowledge was with us – as we took our Vows.

Not surprisingly, by consensus, Terra Novans chose the Tree of Life as Terra Nova's collective symbol, and the colors of green and silver. Green is for growth on the planet; silver stands between the polarized states of black and white. Silver is the "middle pillar," or "trunk" of the Tree of Life.

The path into Terra Nova is simple: Terra Novans ascribe to a Vow anyone can take. Too, anyone can join the Terra Nova Seminary at anytime from anywhere in the world. And, anyone, without attending the Seminary, can join the Terra Nova Alliance.

Terra Novans espouse a Creed of Love.
Terra Novans live by a Code of Honor.

Beyond that, Terra Novans create personal Vows and immerse in personal Causes that help seed our social and moral order with new, healthy, and life-sustaining values.

Terra Nova is held together by the drive to seed our Earth with Synergistic Consciousness: the productive sharing of energy and expertise using collaborative, partnership-based models.

In our Terra Nova Alliance, we strive to remember and celebrate, again and again, our One People, One Spirit, One Earth.

To learn more about becoming a student in the Terra Nova Seminary, please log onto www.pamelaeakins.net
Classes begin the first of every month.

THE TERRA NOVA VOW

I Vow to strive toward
Self-Liberation, Self-Expression, Individuation, and the continuing remembrance of, and care for,
the Ubiquitous Divine Field that exists within and around
All That Is.

I Vow to help others attain
Self-Liberation, Self-Expression, Individuation, and the continuing remembrance of, and care for,
the Ubiquitous Divine Field that exists within and around
All That Is.

May all beings everywhere be free from suffering.

May all beings everywhere be happy.

May I dedicate my life to making it so.

Please join us! Take this Vow, and become part of the Terra Nova Alliance. Please contact us to become an Official Member:
www.pamelaeakins.net

The Terra Nova Vow is reprinted from *Blindness and Sight: A Memoir*, p. 117-118.

THE TERRA NOVA CREED

Love embraces all religions.
Love embraces all nations.
Love embraces all genders.
Love embraces all races.
Love embraces all classes.
Love embraces all ages.
Love knows no bounds.

From *Blindness and Sight: A Memoir*, p. 117-118.

THE TERRA NOVA CODE

I honor the wonder of life and believe that life is sacred.

I honor the individual's direct experience and interpretation of the sacred.

I honor deep contemplation of the meaning of personal and collective life, and believe that such reflection is essential to attaining a balanced individual and social state of being.

I honor considered and conscientious understanding, thought, speech and action.

I honor and celebrate diversity in lifestyle and perception. I honor perspectives that unify and integrate.

I honor empathy and kindness.

I honor nonviolent approaches to conflict resolution.

I honor the simple, natural, creative, and responsible life which does not harm or endanger others or the Earth.

I honor the equality of all.

From *Blindness and Sight: A Memoir*, p. 119-120.

THIS I REMEMBER

I Am Cosmos.
I Am the Daughter of Cosmos.
I Am a Woman of Power Walking.
I Am She Who Has Erotomorphic Vision.
I Am She Who Wields the Oracle of the Sacred Symbols.
I Am a Storymaker.
I Am Fashioning the Future.
I Am the Cosmic Mother sending Luminarias down the Stream.
I Am Imago Woman on the Path of
Her Own Return.

I Remember looking for answers, wanting to stop the War, organizing Anti-War Moratoria, cutting black arm bands.

I Remember going to the University, pursuing Sociology, thinking, if not there, where?

I Remember traveling to El Salvador in the middle of the War, being terrified, feeling horror in every direction, and wailing with the Mothers of the Disappeared.

I Remember talking with the Salvadoran doctor who had Jesus in his eyes: He would *live,* even when he died.

I Remember having faith in Political Solutions, then losing faith in Political Solutions.

I Remember being half-blind and seeking Vision in the Vision of others.

I Remember discovering the possibility of a Spiritual Solution: if we could change our values at the very core, maybe we would survive.

I Remember my absolutely unassailable Love for my children, the Future of the Tree of Life.

I Remember stepping earnestly onto the Spiritual Path, becoming active in Women's Spirituality, entering the Interfaith, Nondenominational Seminary, learning about religion, and becoming clear that a change in consciousness is a Mystical Experience, something that cannot be taught.

I Remember working collectively in my community to provide for every single person in need in our geographical stretch.

I Remember becoming practical: teaching Peace Studies and Conflict Transformation in the school district and in the community.

I Remember becoming a Mediator and working with the Courts.

I Remember finding, then losing, my Partner, the Love of my Life.

I Remember realizing that maybe I can't, I won't, save the World from War, or from itself.

I Remember vowing to continue the Work – anyway.

I Remember that societies organize themselves around symbols that are valued. I ask myself: What do you value? What do you want your life to symbolize? I remember having a dream where my broken teeth turned into White Poppies that fell out of my mouth. What was I trying to express? I remember learning that the White Poppy is the symbol for Peace.

I Remember that I am of the Universe, that I am Earth DNA, that I am human, a member of an evolving species, a species which excels at Transmutation – through activating the Power of Symbolization.

I Remember I am a Storyteller, and that Storytellers create stability as well as change. Storytellers wield the Art and Science of Symbol.

I Remember that, even though the process of evolution is long, my current time is short; and that the ancient Eakins motto on the family crest reads "Time How Short." The two ravens stand together, presumably perusing the battlefield, holding onto those words, and I think, If not Now, When?

I Remember that I am feeling the passage of time slipping between my fingers. I remember that I am balancing on a dream. The moon is oddly tilted, though slanted in my direction, and I am singing in my sleep the ancient mantra: I Love You and Time is Short.

I Remember I Am Love.
I Remember I Am Peace.
I Remember I am asking *You,* Who *I Am* also: What do *You* want to remember?

All this I remember. All this brought me to where I am today.

What brought *Us* together?

May all beings everywhere be free from suffering.
May all beings everywhere be happy.
May I dedicate my life to making it so.

May we walk in Peace.
May we be Love Walking.
May we Bless and Be Blessed.
May we Come Home – Together.
Together – May we All Come Home.

From *To End the War: A Memoir*, p. 354.

THE PARADIGM OF LOVE

I want to focus on Love. I want to focus on that which unites, not that which divides. I want to learn how to Love. I want to stretch myself into Love.

I *choose* Love.

Therefore, in choosing to Love, I have spent my life – since the War – trying to operationalize that. What has emerged, for me, is a new paradigm to live by. I call this paradigm The Ten Powers of the Universe. The Ten Powers of the Universe translates into the Ten Powers of Love. The Paradigm of Love aligns with all I have created in the *Tarot of the Spirit; Kabbalah and Tarot of the Spirit; The Lightning Papers: Ten Powers of Evolution; Visionary Cosmology: The New Paradigm,* and all my other works. The Paradigm of Love requires a redefinition of that which we take for granted. It goes like this:

1. Definition of Self. Original Being: How we know ourselves. *Love is Born and Awakens in the One.* When we recognize that we are Love awakening, we simultaneously realize that we belong. Finally, we can say: I belong here. I Am made of Universe. I Am Universe evolving the Anima Cosma, the Soul of the Cosmos. I Am meant to Be Here Now.

2. Our Aspirations. Attraction: How we rise into our work, our calling. *Love Beckons. Love calls.* Responding to the call of Love requires that we Love ourselves, even as we Love others. Responding to Love's call requires that we recognize, and take responsibility for, our innate cosmological gifts, and that we recognize and celebrate the

unique cosmological gifts of others.

3. Our Imagination. Creation/Emergence: How we give birth to new ways of knowing. *Love Begets Love.* We can imagine and create an integrated/integral world that cherishes, sustains, and celebrates diversity.

4. Our Systems. Stabilization: How we stabilize in the midst of movement. *Love Nurtures Love.* We can create security systems that promote happiness.

5. Our Methods. Cataclysm: How we address pain, suffering, old age and death. *Love is the Courage to Change. Love Heals.* We can imagine and create collective, love-based responses to human suffering.

6. Our Strategies. Synergy: How we work together. Each of us offers our gifts, and the whole becomes greater than the sum of its parts. In that way *Love Embraces the Heart of All.* This requires a long-sighted, process-based focus. Success is defined as participating with all of the Earth communities – human, animal, and environmental – to create a vibrantly healthy way of life.

7. Our Response. Transmutation: How we deepen. We willfully immerse into a more expansive Vision. We seek ways in which *Love Transforms the Universe.* This requires continually searching for meaning, and continually adapting, in order to live a vibrantly alive day-to-day visionary experience – in the midst of on-going change.

8. Our Institutions. Symbolization: How we encode our experience so that we can pass it on. We *Encode Love in Arts and Cultures* – as we imagine ever new ways of being and becoming. We are practicing the creation of new symbols, building a new symbology, that promotes our continuing healthy evolution.

9. Our Internalized Personal and Collective Values. Absorption: What we absorb matters. What we absorb collectively matters. *Love Remembers Love. Love remembers to Love.* We are internalizing values that honor, heal and sustain ourselves and our community.

10. Our Sensibilities. Radiance: *Love Shines! The Universe is Resplendent!* We are radiating cosmic beauty. We are participating efficaciously in

the evolution of the Cosmos. This enhances our sense of meaning, and provides us with an inalienable sense of belonging.

From *To End the War: A Memoir,* p. 362.

MY RELIGION IS LOVE

I hold the golden thread of Love. Now I know: The name of my religion is Love. Love comprises the essential seed and the essential flowering of all religions, Eastern, Western, Indigenous, and Universal.

We enter the mystery of Love through all forms of veneration. The perception of Beauty, for example, can startle us into awakening to Love. To enter deeply into Love is to enter into the sacred mystery of Creation. As we experience the sacred heart of Creation, the mystery of Love concomitantly deepens within us.

To live inside the mystery of Love is to live from the inside out, to live from the "innermost." Masonic journeyer, Manly Hall, once wrote, "We can conquer the furthermost and remain creatures alone and afraid, but when we allow our hearts and minds to be conquered by the innermost, the long journey comes to an end."

Living from the innermost awakens our sense of Cosmic Mystery. Realizing the Cosmic Mystery opens the portal of Faith, and, as the Miracle of Faith blossoms, we find ourselves immersed in the experience of living the devotional life.

I cannot speak for all, so I shall speak for myself. This is what I have learned: Faith is the conscious and voluntary acceptance of the Wisdom, Love, and Security behind and within the process of Creation. It is the recognition of universal integrity. Christians refer to Faith in God. Buddhists describe Faith as confidence in one's own and others' abilities to wake up to the deepest capacity to Love and Understand.

One who lives inside the deep experience of Faith becomes a living chalice. As the container of the Mystery, she experiences the Divine Sacrament within the heart of her own being, even within the heart of her every cell. Manly Hall called this the Heart Doctrine of Christianity. The fact of Presence, he said, is fulfilled by the face of Presence.

Buddhist monk, Thick Nhat Hanh, says, "When we look into the heart of a flower, we see clouds, sunshine, minerals, time, the earth, and everything in the cosmos." Looking into the heart of a flower, we are truly witnessing the *inter-being* of all things. When we understand the nature of inter-being, all barriers dissolve, for, without comprehensive inter-being, life – as we know it – would not exist. Beauty, as we know it, would not exist.

Each of us is, likewise, a flower in the garden. Each of us is made of the whole Cosmos. Each of us, made of Cosmos, is not less than Cosmos itself, nor are we more than Cosmos.

Realizing that we, ourselves, are the nature and heart of cosmic inter-being awakens our desire to witness and celebrate the glorious Mystery. We are Cosmos with the eyes to see itself. We are Cosmos with the ears to hear itself. We are Cosmos with the heart to feel itself. We are Cosmos with the mind to reflect upon its own becoming. We are Cosmos with the power to dream its own future.

This wisdom is the soul of mysticism, that which resides in the heart of all mystics.

For Christian mystics, Christ is the revelation of the Love of God: the immanence of Divinity. The Divine simply exists – by the simple fact of its being. The mystical experience is the direct realization of the truth of Cosmic Existence, the realization of The Real.

As Christian mystics enter Union with God, Buddhist mystics enter Nirvana. Whether called God or Nirvana or Truth or Cosmos, the Living Presence is contained in inter-being. In inter-being, all that is, is United.

I call the Living Presence "Love." Love is the supreme unifier. Love unites what fear divides. As Socrates said, two-and-a-half millennia ago, Love is the most important thing to live for, the means and the end of existence. Love, he said, is the force most powerful. "No force or form of passion can overpower Love, and, when it comes to courage, even the God of War is no match for the God of Love."

Love congeals. Love unites. We are ready to serve Love instantly, even when no force is leveraged upon us.

To enter Love is to serve the eternal Mystery. To reside in Love is to reside inside the mystical state. The mystical experience is an act of unfolding, an act of becoming, even as the flower becomes.

By whatever names they call you, you, too, are the heart of Love. Like a flower you are made of the whole Cosmos. You are not less than Cosmos. You are not more than Cosmos. Awaken to Love and enter into the deepest Mystery of Being and Becoming. Enter the Heart of the Mystery, awaken to the celebration of Love – and begin to experience your life as seeding our ever-expanding garden.

From *To End the War: A Memoir*, p. 338.

WHAT IS RELIGION?

We think of religion as a system of devotion, of observance, a set of attitudes, beliefs, and practices. Our religion encompasses our worldview, our cosmological worldview, the way we are told Being became and becomes – and all the rules, roles, rituals and routines that accompany that.

The world "religion" comes from the Anglo-French *religare,* which means to "tie back." Religion relegates and regulates us. In so doing, our religions attempt to create a sense of safety in a world of chaos, and a social system within which we might better survive. Our religions also attempt to protect us from ourselves.

"Rely" has the same root as "religion." To rely on something means we depend on it. It means we have confidence that something is going to work. Hopefully, our religion offers us a system we can rely on.

In the best case scenario, religion "ties" us into our Cosmos in a deeply meaningful way. In the best case scenario, religion guides us into the heart of the Cosmic Embrace. Religion can enliven us, enspirit us, perhaps even open us to the experience of bliss or ecstasy. Our religion can point to the way into awakening into a mystical reciprocity with the Living Universe that exists within and all around us. Our religion can teach us how to celebrate.

I ask you, truly, should our religions *not* enliven us? Should we *not* be more liberated by religion than bound? We live inside a Universe of mystery, of wonder. Should our religion not liberate us into creative cosmological participation? Should our religion not free us into inspired interbeing?

My religion has become the totality of my cosmological awakening. My religion has become the story of my being, the story of my becoming.

Now, my religion is my beating heart pulsing with the breath of the sea. My religion is the breath of life floating among the redwoods. I touch the gnarled bark and receive the rich effulgent exhalation – exaltation – from the pores of ancient planetary being. My religion breathes like the scent of jasmine wafting across my desk and releasing through the tip of my pen.

My religion has become the Breath of the Eternal.

Converted, my hours have become wings that soar through galaxies.

I hear Raven calling out "I Love You" – and my heart catches fire.

I worship in my Temple, my Temple: this body, this mind, this heart, this spirit, this home, this Earth, this Universe. All I need to do to get there is To Remember. When I Remember, I Awaken. Then every moment becomes a new dawning, the dawning of Spiritual Love and Light. With every new dawning, I come Home again.

When I am Home, I am tied into, intertwined with All That Is, within and without.

There is a trick to Remembering though. To Remember, I have to remind myself to "Wake up!" I have to say to myself, "Wake Up!" And, is that simple command not contained in the astounding power of prayer?

ENTERING THE TEMPLE

Can we change the world through thought? I say, Yes. When we "think", our consciousness becomes focused. Through thinking, we can set our intention. The 14th Dalai Lama once said, "If we have a mind, we should be able to attain happiness." He meant that it is possible to reason our way, or "meditate" or "contemplate" our way, into a desired state of being within ourselves – a peaceful way, a contented way, a way of being part of the solution – even if we are technically in a state of poverty or even inside a war. It may not be easy, but it is possible.

When we find that place within ourselves, it can radiate out into our world.

We seek that place through entering the Invisible Temple – and concentrating our efforts. We can enter the Inner Temple, that which exists within ourselves, and there, discovering we are no more and no less than Cosmos itself, we can likewise become part of the Planetary Temple, the Galactic Temple, the Intergalactic Temple, the Universal Temple. Within the Temple, consciousness, and the potential for consciousness, ever resides. Consciousness is ubiquitous – and evenly distributed – throughout every form from the greatest to the tiniest, and throughout every constituent part of every form. Consciousness permeates All. And, consciousness is not only embodied in form, but disembodied. Consciousness is the ubiquitous potential that thrives throughout the Field.

As humans, we can "aim" our consciousness. We can make our consciousness intentional. We can enter the Temple, simply by thought, and set our intentions on rising into a more exalted state and way of being. Whatever we discover there, will, of course, change us. Whatever we discover there will radiate outward through our changed attitudes and behaviors.

I believe human consciousness is species consciousness. We are like a flock of birds, winging this way and that. Thought alone can drive our patterns. Thought alone can drive our flow.

This does not mean that we will not compete at the feeder, by the way. It does mean, however, that we strongly influence each other by what we think, do, and say – everyday.

When we set our intentions on an idea, we can not only project that idea out "psychically", but we, ourselves, are changed by our own changing focus. Whatever we focus on, whatever we absorb, whatever we consume, is what we become. What we become influences the winged artistry of the flock.

I seek, in my meditations, to focus on Love. Love is the greatest power in the Universe. Love has the power to unite. Love unites that which seems divided. Love is the great receiver. Love takes in graciously. Love stands under – and therefore understands.

Love, however, seems like a complex concept to us. The thought of Unity seems complex.

Therefore, in my focus, in my studies, in my writings, in my teachings, I seek to "operationalize" Love. To operationalize Love is to create ways and means by which Love can be understood and enacted. I wish to be and do Love. I want to Be Love Walking.

To find the Way, the Way of Love, to Be Love Walking, I go into my Inner Temple. I enter my Temple with the full intention of finding Love and filling with Love: Cosmic Love. I meditate, I contemplate, I pray. Through these actions, I attempt to "draw in Love", to "breathe in Love." *Then, hopefully,* I think to myself, *I will be able to breathe more Love into the world – because I do believe Love is the answer. Ask any question;* I say to myself, *Love is the answer. That is what I believe. Love, just Love, can save our ailing planet.*

This action of entering the Inner Temple, and focusing my attention and intention, becomes my spiritual practice. My spiritual practice is just that: Practice. Practice is what we do when we are trying to remember something, or when we are trying to get better at something. Practice means I am trying to learn.

I remember my son's baseball coach saying "There's no such thing as a perfect game. Too many things can go wrong. But there is such a thing as a perfect practice." Perfect, in this case, as the coach was well aware, encompasses all the imperfections of practice – since practice, by definition, is an attempt to improve.

And, so, I will continue to practice. I will continue to observe within the Inner Temple. And, I will attempt to rise from there into the Intergalactic Temple. I will attempt to arise into Universality with a Heart Full of Love. And, I will seek you there, Beautiful One – in that rarefied place. I will search for you there, Precious One – in that World of Beauty. And, together, Beloved Friend, we will wing through the galaxies, full with the Light and the Healing and the Power of Love.

61 FIVE-MINUTE MEDITATIONS TO OPERATIONALIZE LOVE

Tina says, We need to meditate together.
Tina says, Our meditations ought to focus on operationalizing Love, since operationalizing Love is our purpose in the Terra Nova Alliance.
Tina says, There is power in meditating on the same concept.

In the Western Mystery Tradition there is a practice known as Thursday Night Meditation. I don't know how long this observance has been going on, perhaps for hundreds of years. On Thursday night at 7:00 or 8:00 (sometimes 9:00), people meditate silently in their time zone. Even as that thought-based power surges into the body, mind, heart, and spirit of the meditator, this practice causes a wave of thought-based energy to sweep around the planet. Meditation alters us, even as it alters our world. Our world shifts, not only as a result of intentional thought falling down like rain across the planet, but because meditation has the power to change each individual meditator's perceptions. As we think, so we are. Therefore, intentional sustained meditation results in changes in perceptions of personal rules, rituals, roles, and routines. Such a shift cannot help but alter the meditator's environment as the results of intentional meditation radiate outward into manifold aspects of daily life.

Tina believes that thoughts do travel, by the way. And, so do I. Oftentimes, for example, when I visualize a friend or family member I would very much like to speak with, even someone I have been out of touch with for a very long time, when I contemplate that person with intention, soon the phone will ring and it will be that person. How does that happen? We might call that some kind of "psychic communication." Psyche means soul. Somehow, our thoughts catch a cosmic wave of universal soul and ride it out unto their destination. Perhaps our thoughts travel on "strings", perhaps via "loop quantum gravity."

From time immemorial, there have been those who have known this. Thousands have sat in monasteries and prayed for healing. In my book *Kabbalah & Tarot of the Spirit,* I relay the story of the Maryknoll Sisters in Guatemala. Right in the middle of the war, these nuns reclaimed a desecrated church building – which had been used for horrible forms of torture – and turned it into a sacred refuge. They transformed this building of terror into a house of prayer. In the midst of chaos, they created a sanctuary in which all comers were welcome. The Sisters sat through the war praying. As they transmitted their meditations, they transmuting a legacy of misery into a legacy of Light. This is the power of intention. Our thoughts fall down like rain.

So, how shall we set our intention? Upon what shall we focus? What shall we absorb – and what will, concomitantly, consume us?

One day, very recently, I was surprised to find sixty-one meditations in my in-box. These meditations, sent to me by Tina Freimuth – Artist, Visionary Cosmologist, and Terra Novan – were mysteriously comprised of my own words. "Here," Tina wrote, "are 52 weeks of meditations that operationalize Love. We can do these together – globally – on Thursday nights. They are based on your "Ten Powers of the Universe" publications. The meditations are meant to be food for thought. They are sound bites for consciously connecting together for five minutes, weekly, at the same hour, on the same day, world-wide. I see this as the Cosmological Revolution operationalized. This is the New Paradigm."

I am grateful to Tina for her gift – which I now share with you.

I invite you to enter these meditations in your own way, but, for those who are interested in receiving more direction, I offer a method by which you might begin and end your contemplations.

First of all, keep in mind that these meditations were created to be short – eminently doable anywhere at any time. But, of course, we know that meditation, itself, can be a glorious experience, prayer can be a glorious experience, and therefore we may prefer a more elaborate contemplation. When we meditate, when we pray, we expand our consciousness into the consciousness of the Living Cosmos. When we meditate, when we pray, we enter into the Cosmic Temple, that invisible sacred space that lives within and all around us. There, we engage not only with our deepest self, but with all those who are in attendance – exactly at that very hour we have passed through those "doors." We find ourselves connecting, too, with the energies of all who have ever inhabited the Cosmic Temple, and even those who are yet to come.

Here is a suggested meditational format: At 7:00 on Thursday evening, sit quietly. Breathe in the effulgent Universe. Breathe in the Living Cosmos. Feel the powers of the Living Cosmos filling your body, your mind, your heart, and your spirit. Imagine yourself becoming renewed and energized by the living lifeforce of the Universe. The air we breathe sustains us. It is rich with the enlivening essence of chi, ki, prana, pneuma, ruach, Spirit. The universal spark of life, the fiery breath of Spirit, thrives within and all around us. As you feel that energy come alive inside you, as you feel it begin to travel through and awaken in your body, imagine that you are entering the invisible Cosmic Temple. Inside the Cosmic Temple, imagine yourself interconnecting with the countless others with whom you are walking the Path. Imagine this – and it will become. Contemplate, then, the meditation for the particular evening – the particular Thursday of the particular week of the particular month. Imagine the contents of that meditation becoming activated in your consciousness. Imagine all of that – and it will become. Contemplate the meditation, then, until you feel complete. Then, add to your meditation anything you wish to pray for or dream into the Universe. End with a prayer of gratitude. When we inhabit a state of gratitude, our mental state becomes one of appreciation. Appreciation is central to the operationalization of Love. Indeed, I end all my personal meditations, and all my days, with the simple mantra:

        Thank You. Thank You. Thank You.

WEEKLY MEDITATIONS TO OPERATIONALIZE LOVE

JANUARY

Week 1: Welcome to Terra Nova – New Ground, New Thought, New Frontier, New Earth. Welcome to the journey of Being Becoming. Our Mission, together, is to become Creators of the Field and Stewards of the Garden. Together, we are waking up. Together, we are evolving our human consciousness. Together, we are evolving the sensibilities of our species in and as our Earth Community. (*Terra Nova,* p. 7)

Week 2: In 1923, with the new Hubble telescope, we found out that what we thought was a nebula was a galaxy! It turned out to be our Sister Galaxy, Andromeda. *We were not alone.* We *are* not alone. Think of that: up until that moment, we seemed to be an isolated planet. On July 20, 1969, we saw "our Mother's" portrait broadcast for the first time from the moon… She is our amazing biosphere! Let us become Reverent! Exactly because, with our new sense of Place, Space and Time, *we* realized that not only is the Universe not as we thought it was, but we are not who we *thought* we were either. We just *knew* – in our bones – things had changed. (*Terra Nova,* p. 8-9)

Week 3: We are in a New Place and a New Time. We have realized that the Universe is not "up there" somewhere, not "out there" somewhere, but within and all around us. (*Terra Nova,* p. 7)

Week 4: Today, we sense a Big Call. It is a Call to think differently, even if we can't make out clearly what that means or what it might entail. Our Big Call applies to the way we reconceptualize, reinterpret, and reformulate our understanding of our Universe. (*Terra Nova,* p. 9)

Week 5: What we think, say, and do matters. Our Future depends on our process. And, as we are carried by our planet, our planet, concomitantly, carries on within the realm of our understanding. Therefore, our thinking matters. Our ideas matter. And, given the influx of possibilities, what we choose to believe makes all the difference in the world. (*Terra Nova,* p. 9)

FEBRUARY

Week 1: It took 13.73 billion years of universal artistry for our Universe creating, combining and recombining its elements and energies to evolve into You! Even though you share 99.9% of the same DNA as all other human beings, the 0.1% of the DNA code that makes you unequivocally YOU, makes you *absolutely original.* The You that exists right now, in this present moment, has never been before and will never be again. (*Terra Nova,* p. 12-13)

Week 2: The Next Frontier for humanity is, and will be, rending the veil of consciousness. This is A Process for creating Social Change. (*Terra Nova,* p. 1)

Week 3: I feel like I am one of the people called to examine human ideas, one of the people called to try to see things differently, one of the people called to try to bring in new philosophy. And, I am not alone on this path. There must be thousands of us, or, on this planet of close to eight billion people, perhaps we are more than millions. (*Terra Nova,* p. 2)

Week 4: Terra Nova is held together by the drive to seed our Earth with Synergistic Consciousness: the productive sharing of energy and expertise using collaborative, partnership-based models. And, anyone can join the Terra Nova Alliance. (*Terra Nova,* p. 38)

Week 5: I want to focus on Love. I want to focus on that which unites, not that which divides. I want to learn how to Love. I want to stretch myself into Love. I *choose* Love. Therefore, in choosing Love, I have spent my life trying to operationalize that. What has emerged, for me, is a new paradigm to live by. I call this paradigm the Ten Powers of the Universe. The Ten Powers of the Universe translate into the ten Powers of Love. The Paradigm of Love requires a redefinition of that which we take for granted. (*Terra Nova,* p. 46)

MARCH

Week 1: I hold the golden thread of Love. Now I know: The name of my religion is Love. Love comprises the essential seed and the essential flowering of all religions: Eastern, Western, Indigenous, and Universal. (*Terra Nova,* p. 49)

Week 2: Earth was born out of the Sun which was born out of the Milky Way which was born out of the Universe which may have been born out of a multiverse. It's so much bigger than we thought – which changes everything about who we think we are. *(The Lightning Papers,* p. 11)

Week 3: If you take a single atom and blow it up to the size of a pumpkin, the combined matter inside the atom wouldn't even amount to the size of a pumpkin seed. The matter inside each atom occupies less than a tenth of a percent of the atom and the rest of the space is a living field of creative energy. You are actually made *primarily of space.* You are a packet of the Panoriginal Field walking! *(The Lightning Papers,* p. 13)

Week 4: Three thousand years ago in India they were already saying that everything in existence is permeated with the subtle essence. They said the essence was the eye of the eye, ear of the ear, self of the self. They said it's like salt dissolving in water. You can't see it, but you know it exists because you can taste it. *(The Lightning Papers,* p. 13)

Week 5: I want you to wake up. I want to see your eyes sparking with life. I want to see your soul ablaze with fire. I want you to wake up to *cosmological presence*, to realize you *are* cosmological presence, to realize *you are universe in the process of its own self-discovery. (The Lightning Papers,* p. 18-19)

APRIL

Week 1: A worldview breathes like air. We don't even realize we're living by it unless the integrity of that worldview becomes tainted, unless the air we're breathing becomes toxic. We're choking in the malignancy of a culture gone insane. *(The Lightning Papers,* p. 20)

Week 2: Atoms are continuously producing bundles of light that pop into and out of existence. The universe is made of atoms. We are made of universe. Therefore we are made of bundles of light. Like the zero point energy field, neither the individual human nor any human culture is static or inert. The individual human is a continually changing, living, growing, originating *"entity". (The Lightning Papers,* p. 29)

Week 3: It is important to remember, humans are a most adaptable and creative species. We can live and have lived in any and all conceivable circumstances, patterns and arrangements. We contribute to creating our living situation moment by moment. Whatever each of us thinks, says and does every minute of every day flows into the totality of the collective consciousness and impacts "the way it is". Whatever each of us is up to matters – *absolutely. (The Lightning Papers,* p. 30)

Week 4: Here is something to consider: Two types of fools have been identified: the foolish fool and the Great Fool, both of whom may, from the outside, seem ridiculously inept. Here is the difference between the two: The foolish fool is an unconscious bumbler. The Great Fool bumbles conscientiously. *(The Lightning Papers,* p. 31)

Week 5: Your body is composed of a very specific constellation of molecules – oxygen, carbon, hydrogen, nitrogen – that exist very specifically on the planet Earth. You are a modification of a planetary code, Earth's DNA. You share 99.9% of the same DNA with every other human, yet the unshared 0.1% of the code makes you completely distinct from every other human that has ever been or ever will be. A mere 0.1% accounts for your height, your physique, even your talents and your aptitudes. That 0.1% enables the excitement of originality. *(The Lightning Papers,* p. 53)

MAY

Week 1: You are one of a kind. You emerge as a singular presence, an original being. There has never been another you before and there never will be again. This is your moment, your moment to contain and move universal creation. You are a creative center of universe, universe with the power to originate its own future. The unique constellation of you! That is the miracle! *(The Lightning Papers,* p. 54)

Week 2: You are an original flower in the garden. You were meant to be here, in this exact place and time. You were meant to be here because the universe created the exact conditions to bring you forth. You emanated from the origin of existence itself, and you yourself are an original originator. Assume your true identity as an original cosmological presence. Become a full participant in the gift of your moment. Do not imagine that anything in this life is rote. *(The Lightning Papers,* p. 55)

Week 3: Imagine the cosmic sea as dark fluid and the cosmic fire as the basis for luminous matter. Imagine that the products of the universe are ever changing, but that the process of the universe is forever. Truth remains truth and the essence of truth is contained like a seed element throughout the world's philosophies and religions. *(The Lightning Papers,* p. 76)

Week 4: The Cosmological Power of Attraction pervades all things in the universe. We remain on the Earth because of the gravitational attraction between earth and our bodies. Even beyond that, each of us is an electromagnetic field. We move through the cosmos as a unit of centrated mass which is capable of experiencing extreme attraction anytime, anywhere, in any given split-second. *(The Lightning Papers,* p. 99)

Week 5: The ignition that accompanies attraction is physical and emotional, and no emotional experience is stronger for us than love. Love can happen instantly. In a lightning flash, love can become the thing we live and die for, the organizing principle of our lives. *(The Lightning Papers,* p. 99)

JUNE

Week 1: We are living inside a cosmological love story. Awaken, enter, and grasp the tale of your becoming. And, remember, as the masters of old have said, that to which you are drawn has been calling you from the start. *(The Lightning Papers,* p. 101)

Week 2: Not only do we look different from one another, each of us has been endowed with a special complex of attractions that no two people, not even identical twins, could ever share. That's what makes the experiment of the universe so exhilarating. We are participating in a cosmic adventure that keeps unfolding through the Power of Attraction. *(The Lightning Papers,* p. 114)

Week 3: It took 13.7 billion years of universal creation before Beethoven could create the *Ode to Joy*. *(The Lightning Papers,* p. 114-115)

Week 4: The universe is always deciding what to keep and what to discard. It is all about values, what the universe values. That's why each of us needs to have a vision. *(The Lightning Papers*, p. 116)

Week 5: Cosmological becoming is the focus of cosmology. Cosmology is the art of articulating the evolution of creation: how the universe has unfolded and is unfolding. Cosmology, the study of the "order" of being and becoming (or even its "disorder"), depends upon empirical observation, inductive and deductive reasoning, scientific interpretation, and creative story-telling. *(The Lightning Papers*, p. 140-141)

JULY

Week 1: You were born into and as a generation. A generation is a stage in the succession of natural descent as well as a cohort of people who share the same moment on Earth. You are assembled of the matter and energy that exists in your space and time; your "moment." It could be said you are an assemblage of universe with the power of generation. *(The Lightning Papers,* p. 141)

Week 2: I halt at the edge of the forest. I stand, awestruck, blinking, witnessing the glory of the mighty oak, giving birth to seven thousand leaves all in one moment. I want to praise this universe. I want to fall on my knees, bear witness, and give thanks for this extraordinary beauty. In the same moment, I realize I am universe itself, no more and no less than the power of creation unfolding. *(The Lightning Papers,* p. 141)

Week 3: We could create a fabulous future based on the dreams we dream today. That goes for each of us as individuals as well as for the species. We just have to free ourselves. We just have to wake up, to break out of our sense of entrapment, to redefine who we think we are. *(The Lightning Papers,* p. 157)

Week 4: We now realize from the point of view of science, what mystics have always known – that the universe is alive, that we are made of living universe, and that the universe is intelligent and creative. We will rise into understanding that we are universal intelligence. We will rise into participating consciously with and as cosmological creativity. *(The Lightning Papers,* p. 167)

Week 5: As people wake up to the fact that the universe is not 'out there' somewhere, and that human society, just like the universe, does not exist 'out there' somewhere, but, that, as humans, we make up our world everyday of our lives through the choices we make, we will become empowered to create whole new ways of imagining the future. *(The Lightning Papers,* p. 168)

AUGUST

Week 1: It may be important for us to consider the ways in which we are being educated, and what we consider to be important, as we actively participate in imaging the New Era. *(The Lightning Papers,* p. 187)

Week 2: For better or worse, imagination creates not only the values and priorities of the next generation but the values and priorities of the overarching era as well as the era to come. Eras rise and fall. Generations rise and fall. Within generations, just like every star and starfish, every centrated being dies. Death, the ultimate act of the Power of Cataclysm, is part of the universal plan. Death is intrinsic to existence. The simple truth is that building up and taking down are equal parts of the process of creation. *(The Lightning Papers,* p. 229)

Week 3: Understanding the cosmological powers, and that we, ourselves, contain and are composed of these powers, gives us a new way of thinking, a new way to transcend the limitations of our prior socialization and to begin to imagine ourselves as a new kind of species. Yes, we're from space. Yes, we're from Earth. Yes, we're made of Earth. Yes, we contain the processes and intelligences and powers that give rise to life. Knowing this, we can begin to imagine entering into and participating with the dynamic cosmic processes that are at work within and all around us. *(The Lightning Papers,* p. 260)

Week 4: Humans, who are capable of destroying the rain forest in a geological blink, are also capable of wildly imaginative creativity. Humans have an extraordinary ability to consciously and conscientiously reflect upon what they have wrought, what they desire, what is, what has been, what might be. *(The Lightning Papers,* p. 162)

Week 5: We don't have to accept things as they are. We're capable of imagining, then setting about to create new forms of Synergy, new ways of being with each other, new ways of being with other species, even with Earth itself, and the universe. We – those of us living at this very moment – stand at the cutting edge of the 13.7 billion year evolutionary process. Everything that has happened in the universe has led up to this very moment. We can make a difference. Vision is the key, being visionary. *(The Lightning Papers,* p. 262)

SEPTEMBER

Week 1: If only one person thaws and acts, the tide can turn in the opposite direction. Everybody will surge in to help. One single person absolutely makes a difference. One single person can make the entire difference. I have faith that there will be tens, hundreds, thousands, millions, billions of little individual breakthroughs everywhere. And that these little breakthroughs will create a synergistic tide that will alter the course of future forever. *(The Lightning Papers,* p. 263)

Week 2: I'm part of a planetary social movement. We all are. People are waking up everywhere. Because we're out of time. We have to wake up. We have to immerse in the process of conscious self-reflection and begin to open our imagination. We need to create a synergistic system that heals rather than destroys, cherishes and unifies rather than despises and divides. I trust you will find a way to be in love. *(The Lightning Papers,* p. 264)

Week 3: An ecosystem is a "field" in which a "living" community and "nonliving" environment collaborate to form a *synergistic holomovement.* The ecosystem is a region – with an intelligence, mind or consciousness – of any size or shape, ranging from a crack in a sidewalk to the whole of the Earth. A redwood forest is a great example of an ecosystem in action. An ecosystem is comprised of the synergistic interaction of air, soil, light, temperature, rainfall, and living communities. The components or forces of the ecosystem, working together, produce a synergistic holomovement that is infinitely more elegant, articulate and sophisticated than any one of its constituent parts. *(The Lightning Papers,* p. 270-271)

Week 4: As universe itself in the power of its own creation, each of us has the ability to reflect upon our philosophies and actions. As individuals and as groups we can decide, within existing conditions, how we will take action. *(The Lightning Papers,* p. 279)

Week 5: To begin to create new ideas, new minds, and to build new communities in that image, you can reflect upon your exterior and interior conditions. For those who have eyes to see and ears to hear, every single moment and every single relationship holds the magic of transcendental possibilities. *(The Lightning Papers,* p. 208)

OCTOBER

Week 1: Love is the only true protection. All other forms of protection eventually lead to war. *(The Lightning Papers,* p. 288)

Week 2: Ultimately, love is the only thing worth fighting for, and when you know that, you become a knower of the field. The field is the whole cosmos. *(The Lightning Papers*, p. 289)

Week 3: I think if we meditated on our own thoughts and behaviors, especially emotions like anger, we could be instructed and see how we could go deeper and deeper to find out where the real problems lie. If we did that search with love as our highest value, we would see the whole picture completely differently. *(The Lightning Papers*, p. 290)

Week 4: No matter which direction we choose, it is up to each of us, individually and collectively, to imagine how we will proceed. Individually we will express new possibilities. Together we will embrace ideas and create trends that will, eventually, create the properties by which the New Era will be identified. *(The Lightning Papers,* p. 333)

Week 5: Each of us is born into a complex story that was in progress before we arrived and will continue after we are gone. As we become socialized and educated, our consciousness is shaped. Through immersing in the universe, both symbolic and real, we become "knowers of the field". We begin to realize that we ourselves are the creators of the cultural mythos around, through, and by which our personal and collective lives are organized. We begin to realize that the story of our lives is inherently "alive." *(The Lightning Papers,* p. 377)

NOVEMBER

Week 1: It could be said that you are the state-of-the-art universe in progress; a complex conscious entity of space-time at the cutting edge of its own existence. It could be said that you are a seed of intelligent design with the capacity to respond to the synergistic situation in which you find yourself. And by your own particular actions you are creating the synergistic constitution of the future. *(The Lightning Papers*, p. 378)

Week 2: In the shell of her ear, the ocean whispered, the waters breathed. Beneath the surface, the kelp forest rose and fell. Plants, fishes, animals – all are the Anima Cosma, the moving field of a four-billion-year-old undulating entity. Everything pulses as life's living field, absorbing, evolving, and radiating as it becomes. *(The Lightning Papers,* p. 383)

Week 3: We absorb everything that happens to us. All that happens to us, we become. We become all that we experience, all the happiness, all the love, all the sorrow, all the suffering, and all the pain. We contain it all within us. It lodges in our blood, in our bones, in our minds and hearts, especially in our spirits, which is all about the energy to go on living, to go on dreaming. That's what it means to be human. To contain everything. To contain it all. To hold it all, to recognize that, and to grow through our pain. And, as we learn how to contain all that happens to us, or that we happen into, our soul grows rich. Our soul grows huge. *(The Lightning Papers,* p. 400)

Week 4: Absorption! We absorb what we are born into. We also absorb the aspects of the universe we pay attention to, and what results of our own focus, in turn, gets absorbed by the universe. *(The Lightning Papers,* p. 402)

Week 5: What if we imagine ourselves in the river, and instead of imagining that we are going against the current, what if we imagine that we are flowing with the river, and we catch a current that takes into a faster flow, so that, ultimately, we are moving ahead of the mainstream. And, then, from there we cast the seeds of the future, our symbols – the ones we have thought deeply about and consciously created – into the river. That way we seed the future by impacting the stream of consciousness. *(The Lightning Papers,* p. 405)

DECEMBER

Week 1: Much possibility is within us. If we count back only a thousand years in our heritage, we have a million direct ancestors. Beyond that, we contain the universe back to the beginning. Within our very cells – even within our carbon atoms – we remember the past. We can imagine the memory of the future as well. *(The Lightning Papers,* p. 434)

Week 2: Earth isn't a resource. Humans are inseparable from Earth. Earth is the living synergistic endeavor that gives rise to humans, who, as universe with the capacity to reflect upon itself, have a responsibility to wake up and recognize the truth. *(The Lightning Papers*, p. 440)

Week 3: The Great White Shark has been around for a hundred million years so it's pretty well adapted. Now, the universe is concentrating on exploring this set of processes called humanity, an experiment in conscious self-awareness. The human not only feels, but feels itself feeling, and then communicates its feelings with this amazing range of symbolic languages. And because humans think and communicate symbolically, a human's entire life can become a symbolic representation of whatever the human values. *(The Lightning Papers,* p. 458)

Week 4: Deep and real change usually comes from outside the system. It seeps in from the far edges, the permeable zones. *(The Lightning Papers,* p. 471)

Week 5: We continually emit light, sound, chemical signals and symbols. Perhaps we also emit gravitons that draw objects toward us. Concomitantly, we continually receive such forms of energy and convert them into ever new forms of energy. We transform received signals into feelings, ideas and responses. Then, on the basis of our understanding, for better and for worse, we create, destroy and preserve aspects of ourselves and our world, individually and collectively. *(The Lightning Papers,* p. 488)

YOUR NEW YEAR'S MEDITATION: HAPPY NEW YEAR!

We can create and contribute our songs, our stories and our scripts. We can create and contribute our meals, our medicines and our mathematical equations. We can develop and disseminate symbolic systems by which we can alter the ways we conceptualize ourselves and our world. As individuals and as a collective, we can radiate new dreams into a new world, a dimension that is forever becoming. *(The Lightning Papers,* p. 489)

RADIATING LOVE

The Cosmological Power of Radiance is the way the Universe, or an aspect of the Universe, emerges and radiates from and into the Panoriginal Field. The Universe shines. May I shine – as a Radiant Universe of Love:

As we celebrate our centration as original, originating individuals,
    communities, and as a species,
as we experience and rise into the power of our love,
as we begin to imagine and create the conditions that elicit the new,
as we work to stabilize that which is important to us,
as we learn how to move gracefully through cataclysm and how to
    dismantle that which no longer serves,
as we learn how to participate synergistically as part of the
    Earth/universal community,
as we learn how to deepen in heart, mind and body in order to
    participate with the process of transmutation,
as we learn how to create and wield the symbols that preserve, create
    and transform culture,
as we learn how to absorb and contain the processes and products of
    imagination,
we begin to radiate as the newly transformed human imago, the
    reconstituted individual, community and species that has been
    waiting to emerge from our "imaginal cells" for 40,000 years.

From *Visionary Cosmology: The New Paradigm,* p. 170.

TO END THE WAR

The weapon you are pointing
The weapon that is pointed at you
Will become your Ceremony
Your Prayer
Your Song
And Your Jewel Offering

The weapon we point
Is the one we use
To tear apart our own heart

We need to understand
What we are doing
And why we are doing it
We need to understand in the depths
Of our own soul
Or, we will go crazy
We will split in half
And do wrong

We must purify
We must heal
And we must shield ourselves
From splitting

Here's how to heal
First, we must tell a new story about Ourselves to ourselves
Second, we must affirm and reaffirm
Our goodness
And our good alignment
In the Cosmos
Third, we must consume good things:
Songs, Stories, Prayers, Medicines, Foods
And all this will heal us

We can start by walking into It
Then we can sit down with It
Then we can make an offering to It
Then, becoming satisfied,
It may offer something to us:
A Teaching

The Teaching will bless us
The Teaching will change our thinking
The Teaching will change our speech
Then, our thinking and our speech
Will be Holy

The Teachings will bring us Peace
The Teachings will bring us Happiness
The Teachings will bring us Home

Then all will be well
All is well
Now, We Are Home.

From *To End the War: A Memoir,* p. 368.

PRAYER FOR THE TRANSFORMATION OF THE UNIVERSE

Where there is fragmentation,
may I sow evolving creation.
Where there is alienation,
may I sow communion.
Where there is competition,
may I sow collaboration.
Where there is condemnation,
may I sow enlightened integration.
Where there is bondage,
may I sow liberation.

Where there is desolation,
may I sow compassion.
Where there is anger,
may I sow a wider path.
Where there is hatred,
may I sow a wider view.
Where there is violence,
may I sow the methods of peace.
Where there is fear,
may I scatter the seeds of hope.
Where there is hopelessness,
may I sow inspiration.
Where there is devastation,

may I seek to raise aid.
Where there is illness,
may I sow the healing arts.

Where there is death,
may I sow soulful observation
and the intentional mourning
that redeems despairing hearts.
In the field of transformation,
may I sow cosmological initiation.
In the field of transmutation,
may I sow cosmological jubilation.

Through the wide field of the Universe,
may I sow the Blessing of
Love and Light.
Through the field of evolving Universe,
may I sow the Blessing of Delight.
May I witness universal resplendence in every blade of grass.

May I walk lightly,
sow Original Blessing,
and leave Beauty where I pass.

Thank you. Thank you. Thank you.

From *Kabbalah and Tarot of the Spirit*, p. 791.

THE SACRED TEMPLE

May I live my life as if life itself is a Sacred Temple.
May I enter the Ancient Order of Divine Spirit, Divine Love,
Divine Mind, Divine Life.
May I tend the Garden of the Temple
in Peace, in Love, in Faith,
in Contemplation.
May I contemplate with awe the sacredness of the boundless
Universe: Infinite, Eternal, and Sublime.

May I dwell in the Land of Kindness
Forever.

From *To End the War: A Memoir,* p. 370.

WALK IN BEAUTY

May I walk, may it be Beautiful.
May it be Beautiful before me.
May it be Beautiful behind me.
May it be Beautiful to the right of me.
May it be Beautiful to the left of me.
May it be Beautiful above me.
May it be Beautiful below me.
May it be Beautiful all around me.
May it be Beautiful inside me.

May I walk, may it be Beautiful.

In Beauty, it is ended.

A Traditional Navajo Healing Chant.
See *To End the War: A Memoir*, p. 371.

LOBBING FIREBALLS

Religion is spiritual practice
Spiritual practice is remembrance
Remembrance is awakening the Future
Awakening the Future ignites hope
Hope is faith
Faith is dreaming the Field
Faith is dreaming the Future
  A Future of Reverence
  A Future of Blessing

I awake in the Field
I am dreaming the Field
I am dreaming the Future
I am seeding the Field
I have found the burning point
  Within myself
And I am burning toward it
   Desireless
I am burning toward it
   Fearless

I am burning, and rising again, then
Like the sea of grass
  Which is cut and felled
   And inevitably rises

I rise for the sake of resurrection
I rise for the sake of new reflection

I am rising to the occasion
I am rising for the occasion
I rise in silence to seed
Molding Fireballs of Lightning
Molding them in my hands
Packing Fireballs with Lightning
To lob across the lands
    Fireballs of Story
    Fireballs of Song
    Fireballs of Prayer
    Fireballs full with Blessing
These are the Medicines
I am called upon to jettison
I lob Fireballs from and into
    the Sacred Grove
Calling out loudly
The name of this Lightning is
    LOVE

I am making Fireballs
I am lobbing Fireballs
I am lobbing Fireballs eastward
I am lobbing Fireballs intently
I mean to propagate Lightning
I mean to raise Fields of Wonder
I seed the Field with Lightning

    And, I swear

    There will be Thunder.

From *To End the War: A Memoir*, p. 377.

BECOME A TERRA NOVA CENTER

THE ORIGINAL UNIVERSE

I Was, I Am, I Will Be
Origin without beginning
I am the Matrix, but I am not Matter –
I am the space between the spaces.
Primordial energy
From which all things were born.
I am the field all life was sown into
To wax and wean and bloom and wither
In an ancestral rhythm.
You are in me and I am in you
Through me all beings permeate each other
And are One.
I do not know the time you measure –
Yet I am in every cell of yours.
I am the path on which your thoughts may travel
I am the one who gives your Loving wings.
Come, move with me, I'll move with you,
We'll dance up Life together!
And when you touch me
Know that you're no stranger
To the stars.

Ursula Barshi

Beloved Friend, You are a center of Universe within a center of Universe. The Garden of the Universe is within you and you are within the Garden. The Universal Tree of Life has brought you forth, even as you, yourself, are the Tree of Life initiating its own becoming.

You are of the Earth community, and, yet, you are no stranger to the Stars.

> I wrote in *The Lightning Papers: Ten Powers of Evolution:*
> This is what a child of our species needs to hear: You are loved. We love you. You are a beloved child of the Cosmos, a beloved Cosmic Child. The Universe brought you forth and placed you in its heart. You are the heart of becoming and you have emerged in our hearts.
> Welcome to your home, your garden, your place to be, to grow, to bloom, to flourish, and to thrive. You matter here. You belong. Even as you plant the seeds that grow the Garden of Life, you, too, are the Garden of Life itself.
> You are Creation, and the wonder of Creation is with and within you.
> You, Beloved Child, give comprehension to the Great Mystery of who we have been and who we will become.

I write to you now, Beloved Friend. I write to you as the Cosmic Child. I write to you as the Mother of the Future. I write to you with this message on my mind, with this question in my heart. I ask you: *Do you feel the Call?*

Because I feel the Call, and it is a Big Call. I feel the call to be part of the Cosmological Revolution – and I want you to join me.

Are you called to join with the powers of Creation? Are you called to become part of our Terra Nova Alliance?

I would love to join with you.

The first way you can become involved is to take the Terra Nova Vow on page 39 of this book. Take the Vow seriously. Take it with confidence and with heart. Empower yourself to dedicate yourself to a life of meaning, a life of purpose. If you wish, then, contact us and we will welcome you as an Official Member of the Terra Nova

Alliance. Please note: Terra Nova is not about exclusiveness or constraints. Of course, you will make other powerful personal vows as well.

The second way you can participate is to take classes to learn more about the premises of the Tree of Life and how and why that translates into the Paradigm for the Cosmological Revolution. Please look further via the readings referred to in this booklet. Also, please peruse the following websites:
> www.pamelaeakins.net
> www.tarotofthespirit.com
> www.pacificmysteryschool.com

The third way to join in is to become certified as an Official Teacher of Tarot of the Spirit, Visionary Cosmology, or in the Terra Nova Seminary. Again, please refer to the readings in this book and the websites listed above for information, courses, and applications.

The fourth way to engage is to open an Official Terra Nova Center. That would mean that you would teach classes with a base in the Tree of Life Paradigm – as the whole of, or part of, your offerings. This may also apply to classes such as Art, Writing, Movement, Bodywork, Healing, or Metaphysics – in which you would use the Tree of Life Paradigm as your foundation. Can you visualize the Terra Nova Vow, Creed, and Code posted on your wall? Can you imagine the Tree of Life poster you might be teaching from? The minimum requirement to open a Terra Nova Center is to become a certified Visionary Cosmologist. Strong familiarity with *Tarot of the Spirit* is also recommended. Please refer to the websites above for more information.

The House of Terra Nova is calling you. We are calling. *I* am calling. We are the Terra Nova Alliance – and the Alliance needs you.

We are living in a changing world. We don't have to be at a loss. We can be proactive in creating the change we are seeking. We can do this better together. Not one of us is alone. We Are All Children of the Same Universe.

Beloved Friend, I would love to work with you. I would love to help you plant the seeds of the New Garden in your own local Field.

Will you become a Planetary Teacher?

Will you join me in creating a Universe of Love?

Might we do this work together?

I await your reply. I am prepared to wait a long time.

ABOUT PAMELA EAKINS

Dr. Pamela Eakins is a Storyteller, Sociologist, and Visionary Cosmologist. She is also a Priestess and a Minister. She has taught at Stanford University, the University of Colorado, and the California Institute of Integral Studies. She has written several books including her "Cosmic Quartet": *Tarot of the Spirit, Kabbalah & Tarot of the Spirit, The Lightning Papers: 10 Powers of Evolution,* and *Visionary Cosmology: The New Paradigm.* The "Quartet" is now the "Quintet" with the release of *Terra Nova: Field Guide for the Cosmological Revolution.*

Pamela Eakins is the founder of the Terra Nova Alliance.

To learn more, please visit
www.pamelaeakins.net

and Pamela Eakins' YouTube channel.

For Thou Art the Tree of Life

I AM

I WAS

I WILL BE.

AHAVA

Made in the USA
Columbia, SC
26 September 2019